ENGLISH FOR MEDICAL PURPOSES: SPELLING and VOCABULARY

by Virginia Allum

© English for Medical Purposes: Spelling and Vocabulary by Virginia Allum. All Rights Reserved 2012

ISBN 978-1-4717-6562-9

Contents

Glossary of Terms	4
U.S and British English	5
Why is it hard to spell in English?	13
Silent Letters	14
Spelling Forms	16
Various Spellings for the same sound	21
Homonyms, Homophones and Homographs	28
Medical Homonyms	29
Why bother to spell properly?	31
Consonant Doubling	46
Medical Terminology	54
Apostrophes	62
Compound Words and Collocations	64
Plural Words	77
Uncountable Nouns	86
Use of Definite and Indefinite Articles	88
Use of capital letters	91
Numbers	93
Prefixes	97
Suffixes	100
Common phrases	109
Glossary of Hospital Terms	115

Glossary of Terms

vowels	the sounds of the letters a e i o u
semi-vowel	the letter 'w' when it acts as a vowel e.g. law the letter 'y' when it acts as a vowel e.g. day
consonant	The sounds of the letters : b c d f g h j k l m n p q r s t v x z
consonant clusters	• a combination of 2 or 3 consonants e.g. 'st' , 'spl' • also called blends • of all the possible consonant pairs only 'ng' can never start a word. • only 8 three consonant clusters are commonly used in English. These are : scr spl spr squ str thr shr thw • of these 'squ' and 'thw' are rarely used
digraph	a pair of letters which represent a single sound : ph ch sh th (two sounds)
phoneme	the smallest group of speech sounds in a language
phonetics	the science of making speech sounds
phonics	a method of teaching reading and writing using the phonetic system

Differences between British English and US English

British English	US English

-eable
Both –able and –eable acceptable
likeable
liveable
sizeable
unshakeable
 	
But: believable
  curable
  lovable
  movable
  provable
  solvable
  usable
 	
changeable
knowledgeable
traceable
	-able
	
	likable
	livable
	sizable
	unshakable
	
	believable
	curable
	lovable
	movable
	provable
	solvable
	usable
	
	But: changeable
	    knowledgeable
	    traceable

ae aetiology anaemia haematology haematoma haemorrhoids leukaemia paediatrics paedophile	**e** etiology anemia hematology hematoma haemorrhoids leukemia paediatrics pedophile
-ant / -ent **-ant form used for the noun and –ent used for the adjective** dependant (noun) - dependent (adj)	**-ent** dependent (noun and adjective)

British English	US English
-ce	**-se**
defence	defense
licence	license
offence	offense
pretence	pretense
But: other forms of the words	
defensive	defensive
offensive	offensive
-ce (noun) and –se (verb)	**-ce (verb and noun)**
Rule: Noun –ce and verb –se when the pronunciation of the noun is 's' and the verb is 'z'	**Rule: Noun –ce and verb –se when the pronunciation of the noun is 's' and the verb is 'z'**
advice - to advise	advice to advice
device - to devise	device - to devise
	But: these do not follow the rule
practice - to practise	practice to practice
license - to license	license to license
-ction or –xion	**-ction**
connexion (rarely used)	
connection (more common now)	connection
-t Past tense variation	**-ed Past tense variation**
dreamt	dreamed
learnt	learned
-geing	**-ging**
ageing	aging
ageism	agism
singeing (from singe)	**But:** singeing (singing = singing a song)
But: cringing (from cringe)	cringing
lunging (from lunge)	lunging
syringing (from syringe)	syringing

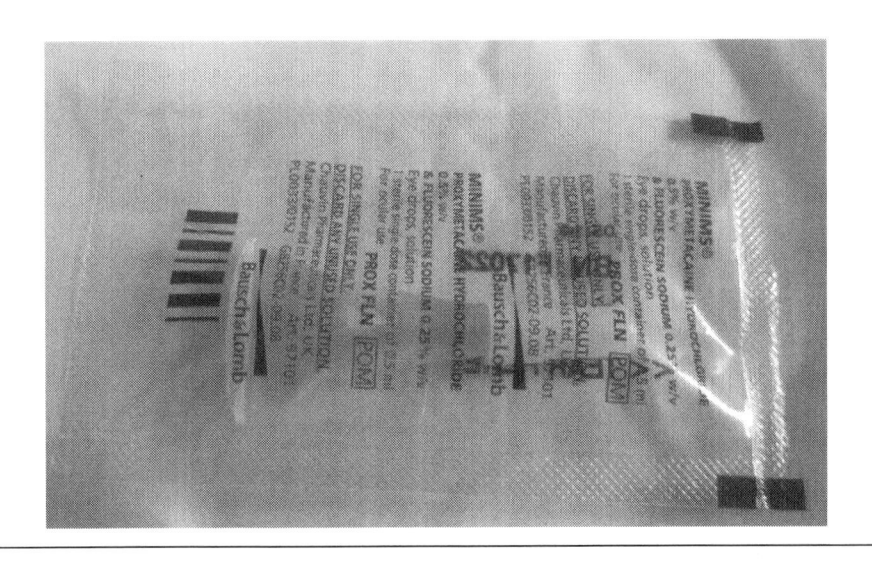

British English	US English
-l	-ll or –l
annul	annul
annulment	annulment
appal	appall
distil	distill
enrol	enroll
enrolment	enrollment
enthral	enthrall
fulfil	fulfill
fulfilment	fulfillment
instalment	installment
instil	instill
skilful	skillful
until	until
wilful	wilful
-ll **Nouns and adjectives** calliper jewellery pupillage woollen	-l **Nouns and adjectives** caliper jewelry pupilage woolen

British English	US English
-ll	**-l**
after –ed -ing -er -est -er -or	**after –ed -ing -er -est -er -or**
bevelled	beveled
cancelled	canceled
counsellor	counselor
cruellest	cruelest
dialled	dialed
dishevelled	disheveled
enamelled	enameled
equalled	equaled
fuelled	fueled
funnelled	funneled
initialled	initialed
labelled	labeled
modelled	modeled
quarrelled	quarreled
signalled	signaled
travelled travelling traveller	traveled traveler traveling
libellous	libelous
marvellous	marvelous
-ll	**-ll**
appalling	appalling
cancellation	cancellation
chancellor	chancellor
compelled	compelled
excelling excellent	excelling excellent
install	install
null nullify	null nullify
propelled	propelled
till	till
tonsillitis	tonsillitis
woolly	woolly (can find 'wooly')

British English	US English
-l	-l
although	although
altogether	altogether
apparel	apparel
bevel	bevel
cancel	cancel
chilblain	chilblain
counsel	counsel
dial	dial
dishevel	dishevel
enamel	enamel
equal	equal
fooling	fooling
fuel	fuel
funnel	funnel
label	label
paralleled unparalleled	paralleled unparalleled
pealing	pealing
perilous	perilous
revealing	revealing
scandalous	scandalous
shrivel	shrivel
spiral	spiral
towel	towel
tunnel	tunnel
welcome	welcome
welfare	welfare

British English	US English
-mme	**-m**
programme	program
gramme (almost obsolete)	gram
oe	**e**
amoeba	ameba
diarrhoea	diarrhea
foetid	fetid
oedema	edema
oesophagus	esophagus
oestrogen	estrogen
But: fetus generally accepted	fetus
-ogue	**-og**
analogue	analog
catalogue	catalog
dialogue	dialog
monologue	monolog
-ould	**-old**
mould	mold
smoulder	smolder
-our	**-or**
Words with an unstressed ending (our)	**Words with an unstressed ending (our)**
endeavour	endeavor
behaviour	behavior
colour	color
favour favourite	favor favorite
flavour	flavor
honour	honor
humour humourless	humor humorless
labour	labor
neighbour	neighbor
savour savoury	savor savory
vigour	vigor
contour	But: contour
glamour	glamour
saviour	saviour

British English	US English
-or glamorous honorary honorific laborious rigor (mortis) vigorous invigorate	**-or** glamorous honorary honorific laborious rigor (mortis) vigorous invigorate
-rior anterior exterior interior superior	**-rior** anterior exterior interior superior
-re calibre centre fibre goitre lustre manoeuvre meagre metre ochre sombre theatre titre	**-er** caliber center fiber goiter luster maneuver meager meter ocher somber theater titer
- er filter meter (measuring instrument) parameter tender	**- er** filter meter parameter tender
- re lucre mediocre	**- re** lucre mediocre
British English	**US English**

British English	US English
-ise	**-ize**
organise	organize
prise (open)	prize (open)
realise	realize
recognise	recognize
-ize	**-ize**
capsize	capsize
euthanize	euthanize
seize	seize
-ise	**-ise**
compromise	compromise
demise	demise
despise	despise
disguise	disguise
excise incise	excise incise
exercise	exercise
expertise	expertise
in the guise of	in the guise of
revise	revise
rise	rise
supervise	supervise
surmise	surmise
wise	wise
- yse	**- yze**
analyse	analyze
hydrolyse	hydrolyze
paralyse	paralyze
British words	**US words**
draught	draft
grey	gray
judgement	judgment
moustache	mustache
sceptic	skeptic
walking aid	gait aid

Why is it so hard to spell in English?

There are many reasons why English is considered one of the most difficult languages to spell. Here are a few:

English is not a phonetic language. In fact, it is called an 'orthographically deep' language because English letters often bear no resemblance to the sounds they represent. Around 90 sounds of English can be spelled in over 200 different ways. This makes spelling very difficult for everyone. The English writing system doesn't match the sound system. There are too many sounds with not enough letters for each sound. Some sounds are spelled in a very strange way e.g 'ph' = 'f'

There have been many historical changes which have given us a rich language (the upside) which is difficult to spell (the downside). Unfortunately, English has never had an Academy to regulate it and Spelling Reform hasn't happened either.

English has a lot of 'empty' or silent letters. English has borrowed from many languages over many centuries. Words were adapted and often changed in some way. One of the adaptations was a change in pronunciation sometimes without removing the letter which is no longer pronounced.

aplomb	gnash	business	mnemonic	ptomaine
comb	gnaw	knack of	Autumn	ptyalin
numb	malign	knee	column	raspberry
succumb	paradigm	kneel	condemn	receipt
thumb	phlegm	knife	damning	February
womb	resign	knock	solemn	iron
muscles	sign	knot	coup	corps
scissors	annihilate	knowledge	corps	debris
handsome	catarrh	knuckle	cupboard	island
sandwich	diarrhoea	almond	psychedelic	vis-s-vis
Wednesday	dishonest	lip-balm	pseudonym	bustle
align	exhausted	calf	psoriasis	chasten
assignment	exhibition	calmness	psychiatrist	epistle
benign	gonorrhoea	could	psychiatry	gristle
campaign	haemorrhage	folklore	psychoanalysis	hustle
consign	haemorrhoids	half	psychogenic	jostle
design	honesty	halves	psychosis	listen
diaphragm	inhibition	palm	psychosomatic	pestle
feign	nihilism	should	psychotic	rapport
foreign	rhythm	stalk	psychotropic	asthma
foreigner	vehement	talkative	psyllium	
gnarled	vehicle	walkover	pterygium	

wholemeal	wretched	wrote
wholesome	wriggle	wrought
wholly	wring	wrung out
whooping cough	wrinkle	faux pas
wrack and ruin	wrist	laissez faire
wrangle	write-off	rendezvous
wrapper	writhe	
wrath	writing	
wreckage	written	
wrench	wrongdoing	

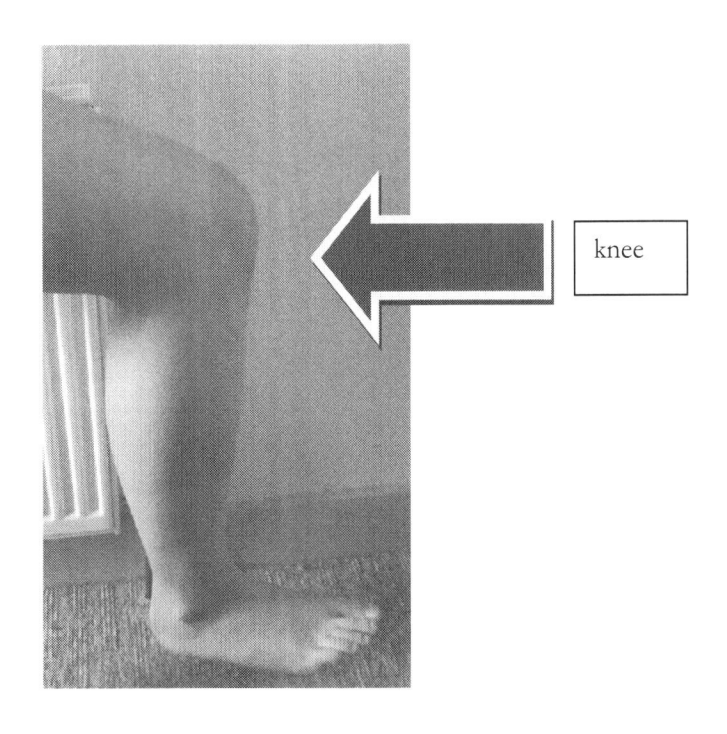

knee

Spelling Rules

There are quite a few spelling rules which can help you even if many have exceptions.

How to spell soft 'c'

-ience	-scence	-ci	-ccy
ambience	acquiescence	acid	coccyx
audience	adolescence	antacid	
conscience	convalescence	flaccid	
convenience	effervescence	lucid	
inconvenience	fluorescence	pellucid	
experience	luminescence	rancid	
inexperience	obsolescence		
obedience	phosphorescence		
patience	reminiscence		
resilience			
science			

Hard 'c'

-cca	-cco	-ccl	-ccu
desiccate	accolade	acclaim	accumulate
impeccable	accommodate	acclimatise	accurate
occasion	accomplish		accusation
saccharin	accordingly		hiccups
	accustomed		occult
	account		occupant
			occupation
			succumb

Hard and soft 'c' and 'g'

Hard c +able	Soft c + able / Soft c + ible	'sh' sound + able	Soft g + able / soft g + ible	Hard g +able
despicable	displaceable	appreciable	changeable	indefatigable
explicable	enforceable	depreciable	chargeable	
impeccable	forcible		dischargeable	
implacable	invincible		exchangeable	
uneducable	irreplaceable		interchangeable	
practicable	noticeable		knowledgeable	
	peaceable		manageable	
	producible		negligible	
	pronounceable		salvageable	
	reducible			
	serviceable			
	traceable			

Rule: 'i' before 'e' except after 'c' when 'ie' says the 'ee' sound

-ie (ee sound)	-ie (i-e separate sounds)	-ei	-ei (e-i separate sounds)
achieve	acquiesce	Alzheimer's	albeit
belief	acquiescence	beige	atheist
believe	alien	caffeine	reimburse
disbelieve	alienate	ceiling	reincarnation
brief	audience	codeine	reinforce
chief-of-staff	anxiety	conceited	reinstate
debrief	client	conceive	reissue
die (dying)	diet	counterfeit	reiterate
field	dietician (UK) dietitian (U.S)	deceitful	
fiend	fiery	deceive	
fierce	lenient	either	
friend	notoriety	neither	
grief	quiet	feign	
grieving	quieten	feint	
hierarchy	quietness	foreign	
hygiene	society	forfeit	
lie (lying)	variety	height	
in lieu of		inveigle	
masterpiece		leisure	
mischief		misconceive	
mischievous		neighbour	

ie = ee	ie = separate sounds	ei = ee	ei = separate sounds
niece	client	perceive	
piece	diet	protein	
pierce	dietician	reign	
reprieve	fiery	receive	
review	hierarchy	receipt	
shield	photocopier	rein	
species	pliers	seize	
tie (tying)	quiet	sleight-of-hand	
vie (vying)	quietness	sovereign	
view	society	surveillance	
yield	supplier	veil	
		vein	
		weigh	
		Zeitgeist	

- CEIVE words

verb infinitive	present participle	past participle	noun	adjective
conceive	conceiving	conceived	conception	well-conceived ill-conceived
deceive	deceiving	deceived	deception	deceptive
perceive	perceiving	perceived	perception	perceptive
receive	receiving	received	reception	receptive

Rule: When you add a suffix which starts with a vowel to a word which ends in 'e', drop the 'e' and add the suffix. Otherwise you have too many vowels together. For example,

like + ing = liking   **But :** agree +ing = agreeing

Rule: When you add a suffix which starts with a vowel to a word which ends in a 'y', change the 'y' to 'i' and add the suffix. For example,

happy + er = happier   happy + est = happiest

carry + s = carries

Exceptions for the 'y to i' rule.		
convey	+s	conveys
key	+s	keys
kidney	+s	kidneys
prey	+s	preys
purvey	+ed	purveyed
survey	+s	surveys

Various spellings for a single sound

Words which use the 'ʃ' or 'sh' sound

-tion	-sion	-ssion	-cion
abstention	compulsion	depression	coercion
adoption	pension	digression	suspicion
assertion	repulsion	discussion	
contortion	torsion	mission	
dictation		obsession	
direction		passion	
discretion		percussion	
fruition		possession	
inhibition		profession	
invention		recession	
lotion		transgression	
motion			
ration			
selection			

Words which use the 'ʃ' or 'sh' sound

-xion	-cheon	-chion	-cian	-shion	-tian
complexion	luncheon	ischion	beautician	cushion	Alsatian
connexion	truncheon	stanchion	clinician	fashion	Christian
flexion			diagnostician		unchristian
reflexion			dietician (UK)		Croatian
			geriatrician		Dalmatian
			mathematician		dietitian
			obstetrician		Egyptian
			optician		gentian violet
			paediatrician		Laotian
			physician		Tahitian
			tactician		venetian

Words which use the 'ʃ' or 'sh' sound

-scent	-tient	-tience	-cient	-ciency
ascent	impatient	impatience	ancient	
convalescent	patient	patience	efficient	efficiency
descent	quotient		coefficient	
effervescent	sentient		inefficient	inefficiency
fluorescent			insufficient	insufficiency
pubescent			omniscient	
reminiscent			proficient	proficiency
			sufficient	sufficiency

Words which use the 'ʃ' or 'sh' sound

-ceous	-cious	-tious	-xious
curvaceous	atrocious	ambitious	anxious
herbaceous	audacious	cautious	noxious
sebaceous	auspicious	conscientious	obnoxious
	delicious	contentious	
	efficacious	facetious	
	fallacious	infectious	
	gracious	nutritious	
	judicious	ostentatious	
	luscious	pretentious	
	malicious	propitious	
	officious	vexatious	
	pernicious		
	precocious		
	spacious		
	specious		
	suspicious		

Words which use the 'dʒ' or 'French je' sound.

-sion	-sion	-sian	-tion
adhesion	explosion	artesian	equation
allusion	immersion	Friesian	
conclusion	incision		
confusion	invasion		
decision	occasion		
division	persuasion		
effusion	protrusion		
erosion	version		
lesion			

Words which use the 'ə' or Schwa sound.

-geous	-gious	-cious	
advantageous	contagious	atrocious	judicious
gorgeous	litigious	audacious	malicious
outrageous	prodigious	conscious	pernicious
umbrageous	religious	delicious	precocious
	sacrilegious	efficacious	spacious
		fallacious	suspicious
		ferocious	vicious
		gracious	voracious

-ious	-ious	-tious	-uous
abstemious	anxious	ambitious	arduous
acrimonious	luxurious	cautious	contemptuous
copious	mysterious	conscientious	continuous
curious	notorious	contentious	fatuous
delirious	noxious	facetious	impetuous
deleterious	obnoxious	fictitious	ingenuous
envious	perfidious	infectious	innocuous
fastidious	precarious	nutritious	presumptuous
furious	previous	ostentatious	strenuous
glorious	rebellious	pretentious	tempestuous
harmonious	semiprecious	propitious	vacuous
hilarious	serious	seditious	virtuous
felonious	spurious	vexatious	voluptuous
industrious	studious		
ingenious	supercilious		
insidious	tedious		
laborious	various		
	victorious		

Dealing with 'gh'

This suffix has several pronunciations which mean that the words don't always follow one particular rule. The reason for this is because the words often have different origins and follow the rules of the original language. For example.

-augh (f)	-ough (f)	-eigh (ay)	-eight (ait)	- ight (ite)
laugh	cough	weigh	eight	bright
laughter	enough	outweigh	weight	fortnight
	rough			light
	slough			mighty
	tough			midnight
	trough			

The 'ought' sounds

-aut	-aught	-art	-ort	-ought
	caught	quart	cohort	ought
	daughter-in-law	stalwart	consort	bought
	distraught	thwart	import	brought
	fraught	wart	report	fought
	naughty		resort	sought
	onslaught		short	thought
taut	taught		sort	
			support	

Homonyms Homophones Homographs

There are many homophones (words which sound the same) and homographs (words which are spelled the same but have different meanings) - these are very confusing. Sometimes the only way to know which word is referred to is by looking at the context e.g 'a sore throat' not a 'soar throat'.

homonyms   words which are spelled the same and pronounced the same but have different meanings   e.g discharge

homophones   words which sound the same but have different meanings e.g roll and role

homographs   words which are spelled the same but have different meanings e.g. wound

It is also important to look at where the stress falls in homographs. This can make quite a difference to the pronunciation of a word. There are also some words which represent both the noun and the verb but with different syllable stresses. An example of this is:

process (noun)   The stress falls on the first syllable

to pro**cess** (verb)   The stress falls on the last syllable

Medical Homophones

Term	Meaning
accept	agree to take something
except	excluding something
access	ability to enter a place
axis	fixed straight line
dying died	present participle of 'die'
dyeing dyed	present participle of 'dye'
affusion	a form of therapy where water is poured over the body as a type of therapy
effusion	escape of fluid into another part of the body e.g pleural effusion
aid	device which helps patients do something
aide	helper or assistant e.g. nursing aide
aids	devices used to help patients e.g walking frame
AIDS	Acquired Immuno-Deficiency Syndrome
aloud	spoken words or sounds
allowed	something which is permitted
assistants	people who help other people e.g medical assistants
assistance	help
bare	without covering, (bare elbows)
bear	tolerate, (bear the pain)
board	piece of wood
bored	have nothing to do
breach	break (old form) e.g. breach of the law
breech	back part e.g. breech birth

Term	Meaning
buccal	relating to the mouth
buckle	something which joins the ends of a belt
callus	hard skin
callous	harsh or unfeeling
cereal	grains, e.g. breakfast cereal
serial	numbers in sequence e.g serial number
coarse	rough
course	series or episode of treatment e.g. a course of antibiotics
complement	go well with
compliment	flattering words
councillor	member of a council e.g. local government council
counsellor	advisor, e.g. marriage counsellor
disc	round plate e.g computer disc
disk	round plate ,interchange with disc
discrete	separate
discreet	avoid embarrassment by using tact
elicit	draw something out e.g. information
illicit	illegal e.g. illicit drugs
feint	not dark e.g feint lines
faint	lose consciousness
foul	dirty
fowl	animals such as chickens
gait	the way a person walks
gate	door which keeps a fence closed

Term	Meaning
glands	several groups of cells which secrete hormones
glans	penis
heal	restore good health
heel	calcaneus, back part of the foot below the ankle
heroin	morphine-like drug
heroine	female hero
hoarse	rough, rasping voice
horse	equine animal
humerus	arm bone
humerous	funny
ilium	upper part of the pelvis, hip bone
ileum	lowest part of the small intestine
inflection	bending forward. Also, inflexion
inflexion	bending forward. Also, inflection
lightening	bleaching, made whiter
lightning	flash of light with thunder
meter	apparatus to measure the quality of something e.g. peak flow meter
metre	Brit. Eng 100 cm
miner	a person who prospects for minerals
minor	a person under a legal age or something which is smaller or less important
missed	past tense of miss
mist	fine spray e.g. nebuliser
mucus	secretion out of the mucous membranes
mucous	adjective form of mucus

Term	Meaning
naval	relating to ships
navel	umbilicus
pain	unpleasant sensation, soreness
pane	framed sheet of glass
passed	past tense of pass
past	previous time
patients	sick people in hospital
patience	being able to wait for something
peak	highest point of something
peek	quick look at something
peroneal	relating to the fibula
perineal	relating to the perineum (pelvic floor)
piece	part of something
peace	feeling of relaxation
plain	obvious, evident
plane	flat, two-dimensional surface
plural	more than one
pleural	relating to the membrane covering the lung
poor	having no money
pore	small opening e.g. pore of the skin
principle	rule
principal	head of a school, the most important
rack	cause great pain e.g. racked with guilt
wrack	destruction, e.g. 'wrack and ruin'

roll	object rolled into a cylinder shape e.g. roll of tape
role	character or part
sac	pouch or capsule
sack	rectangular bag e.g a paper bag
shear	force which causes an opposite, sliding force
sheer	see through or transparent e.g. a sheer blouse
site	location
sight	ability to see
cite	quote someone's words
stationary	standing still
stationery	note-paper
stanch	stop the flow of something e.g. stanch the flow of blood
staunch	strong, steadfast e.g. a staunch supporter
suit	a set of clothes e.g trousers and jacket
suite	a staff of attendants e.g. Birthing Suite
vain	conceited
vein	type of blood vessel
venous	adjective of vein
venus	planet
vesicle	small cyst, usually filled with fluid
vesical	bladder e.g. urinary bladder
waist	area around the middle of the body
waste	unwanted substances

Near Homophones

Term	Meaning
aural	hearing
oral	mouth
bruit	abnormal sound heard on auscultation
brute	rough person
dysphasia	difficulty speaking
dysphagia	difficulty swallowing
legion	a large number e.g. legion of honour
lesion	wound
pharynx	throat
phalanx	long bone of the fingers or toes
tract	long area, passage
track	path

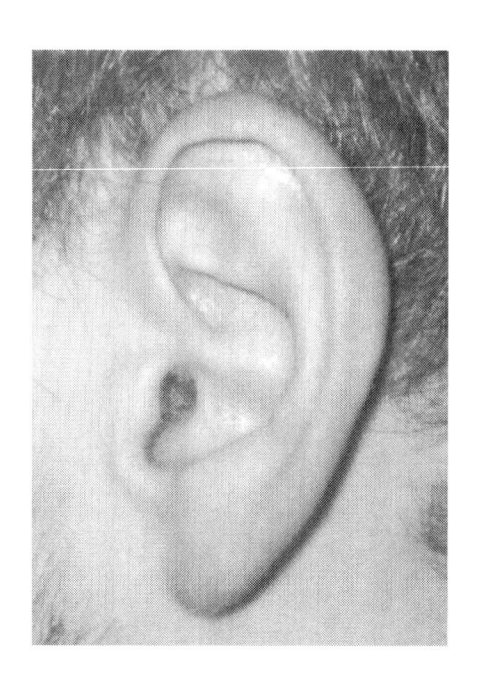

Homonyms

boring	not interesting
boring	drilling into
calculus	hardened dental plaque
calculus	kidney stone
cervix	neck
cervix	neck of the womb (cervix)
cervical	adj of neck
cervical	adj of cervix
cystectomy	removal of a cyst
cystectomy	removal of the bladder
discharge	secretions from a wound
discharge	leaving the hospital for home
lead	rhymes with 'bed'-type of metal
lead	rhymes with 'bead' - opposite of 'follow'
os	mouth e.g. per os (by mouth)
os	bone
medium	average
medium	a particular substance e.g. contrast medium
pelvis	area around the kidney
pelvis	one of the hip bones
screen	curtain or partition used for protection or privacy
screen	battery of tests used to diagnose a disease or condition
wound	a lesion e.g. a cut
wound	past tense of wind ,rhymes with 'sound'

Easily confused words

Term	Meaning
accept	take in, agree to
except	other than
acidic	adjective of acid
ascitic	adjective of ascites
adverse	opposing something
averse	a feeling of distaste
affect	feeling e.g 'flat affect'
effect	bring about a result
allusion	indirect reference to something
illusion	something which appears to be real
assure	make sure, promise a person that something will happen
ensure	make sure, guarantee something
insure	make certain, have an insurance policy
axillary	adj for axilla or armpit
auxiliary	someone or something which helps
bowel	intestine
bowl	receptacle e.g. soup bowl
caries	tooth decay
carries	from the verb 'carry'
choose	select
chose	past tense of 'choose'

cloths	pieces of rags used for cleaning
clothes	garments people wear
conscience	a sense of right and wrong
conscious	alert and oriented
enervate	weaken or destroy
innervate	stimulate a nerve
facies	appearance of the face, e.g. in certain diseases
faeces	stool, bowel movement
farther	at a greater distance e.g. He ran farther today than yesterday
further	extension of time and distance e.g. a further week's treatment
few /fewer	people/objects which can be counted
little / less	small quantity
hanged	criminals are hanged
hung	paintings are hung on the wall
imminent	about to happen
eminent	very important
later	at a time after the present
latter	former
lie lay (past) have lain lying (down)	rest, lie down
lay laid (past) have laid laying	place something somewhere
loath	unwilling to do something
loathe	dislike intensely
loose	make less tight
lose	can't find

moral	ethical
morale	level of cheerfulness people feel
nauseated	feeling sick
nauseous	something which causes nausea or sickness
nutritional	adjective for nutrition
nutritious	something which is healthy to eat
official	something which is authorized or lawful
officious	someone who is over-keen to follow laws or regulations
persecute	harass or oppress a person e.g. because of religious belief
prosecute	take a person to Court
precede	go before
proceed	go on or continue
prescribe	to order a medication for a patient
proscribe	to ban something
prostate	male gland
prostrate	lie down because of emotion e.g. prostrate with grief
quiet	not loud
quite	fairly e.g. quite good
raise	lift up
rise	get up or increase
rational	using the ability to reason or rationalise
rationale	an explanation
serous	adjective of serum
serious	grave or important

Opposite expressions

Term	Meaning
adduct	bring together e.g legs
abduct	move apart
afferent	moves away from a place e.g a central body organ
efferent	moves towards a place e.g a central body organ
anterior	front
posterior	behind
avert	to turn away or ward off e.g. an illness
evert	turn inside out
eversion (foot)	movement away from the imagined central line e.g eversion of the foot
inversion (foot)	movement towards the imagined central line e.g inversion of the foot = twisted ankle
distal	area farthest away from the midline
proximal	area closest to the midline
dorsal	toward the back
ventral	toward the front
elevation	movement upwards
depression	movement downwards
flex	bend
extend	straighten
hypo	low
hyper	high
intra	inside
extra	outside

Term	Meaning
lateral	side
medial	middle
literally	actually, really
figuratively	not exactly but metaphorically
macro	very large
micro	very small
normal	within a standard range
abnormal	out of a standard range
pronation	rotation of the hand or foot towards the floor
supination	rotation of the hand or foot towards the ceiling
scant	small amount of something
excessive	too much of something (sometimes *poly*)
super	over, above
supra	above, upon
superior	situated above e.g the elbow is superior to the wrist
inferior	situated below
supine	lying face up
prone	lying face down
tachy-	fast
brady-	slow

Why bother to spell properly anyway?

Anything you write is judged by its spelling. This is particularly important with academic work. Correct spelling makes it appear that you know what you are writing about. Also, it does not look good to misspell words which occur frequently in your own field of expertise.

Why not just use spell checker?

Spellchecker is a big help if you use it well. Going over your work using Spellchecker before handing it in is very wise as it will pick up most of your spelling errors. Spellchecker's limitation is that it does not differentiate between homophones e.g. a sore throat, not a soar or saw throat.

You can use the Thesaurus feature if you need to check homophones. The Thesaurus will give you a list of words with similar meanings.

The other important thing to do is to set the language which your computer uses to spell check to the appropriate English. If you are studying in the USA, for example, you may like to set the language as US English.

What are the most common spelling mistakes in English spelling?

Interestingly, native speakers (called L1 speakers) and non-native speakers (called L2) make the same five common mistakes. The only difference is the order of making the errors.

The 5 most common mistakes are:

1. Omitting or leaving out letters - around 35% of errors

This often happens with 'double consonants'. The rules for doubling consonants are quite difficult. It is a good idea to make up a table with the rules and add words as you find them. You can then use the table as a quick reference.

2. Substituting or adding in extra letters - around 20 % of errors

This often happens because of the sound of the word. An example of this is substituting the letter 'a' for 'i' in 'definite' (writing 'definate').

3. Substituting whole words - about 20 % of errors

This is also often a result of words which are homophones. Chinese speakers often substitute 'killed' for 'cured' because of the way they tend to pronounce both words to sound the same.

4. Insertion or adding in extra letters - around 20 % of errors

This may be because part of the word is like another word which is spelled differently e.g adding an extra 'l' onto 'beautifull' because of the spelling of the word 'full'.

5. Transposition or mixing up letters - around 5%

This is simply mixing up letters e.g 'freind' instead of 'friend'. Spelling rules are helpful here, however, exceptions to the rule have to be learned as well.

What can you do about it?

Take heart! Even if you omit letters, the meaning is still clear. The meaning should also be clear by looking at the context.

Learn the basic spelling rules. Whilst some people think there are no spelling rules in English – there are. Buy a small notebook and start pages for each spelling rule. Open the notebook to a double page and head one side 'Follows the rule' and the other page 'Exceptions to the rule'. An example is 'Words using 'ie' except after 'c'

Start a list of homophones and homographs in your notebook. Use a Thesaurus to help. Add the meanings to each word. Make sure you add the common errors:

its (of it) it's (it is)

they're (they are)   their (of them)   there (over there)

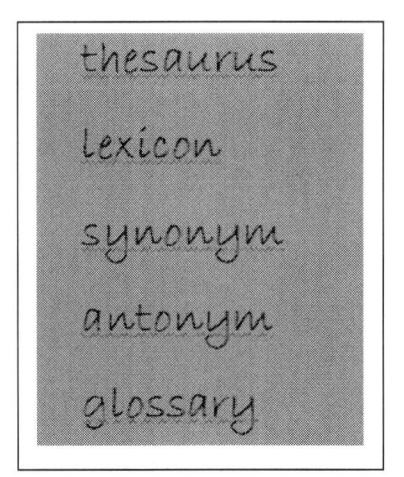

thesaurus
lexicon
synonym
antonym
glossary

Keep a list of words which come up in your studies. Look at the shape of the word, write it out a few times and keep looking at it in your note book. Familiarity helps a lot.

Rules for consonant doubling

Double the consonants in the following words

- in short words which end in a single consonant (except 'x') .For example,

base word	suffix	Term	Example
fur	-y	furry	furry coating
mat	-ed	matted	matted hair
pus	-y	pussy	pussy discharge

- In these words of more than one syllable

format	formatting	formatted
handicap	handicapping	handicapped
program	programmer	programmed

- In words which are formed using Latin prefixes, double the same letter at the end of the prefix. Note: the final letter of the prefix often changes according to the first letter of the base-word.

Prefixes which change a letter for assonance (to sound better)

prefix	prefix family	meaning	Example
a- abs-	ab-	away from, without	asocial abnormal
a- ac- ad- af- ag- al- an ap- ar- as- at-	ad-	towards, near, in addition	adrenal afferent agglutinisation
ant-	anti-	against, opposed to	antagonist
aut-	auto-	self, same	autism
co- col- com- cor- con-	com-	with, together	correlation
de- di- dif- dis-	dis-	1. opposite 2. two 3. exclude	dissimilar
e- ec- ef- ex-	ex-	out of, without, from	exit

prefix	prefix family	meaning	Example
el- em- en-	en-	1. in 2. put in, on, onto	embellish
extra- extro-	extra-	outside, beyond, besides	extrovert
il- im- in- ir-	in-	1. in, on, into, against 2. not	illogical
ob- oc- of- op-	ob-	toward, against, in the way	obstruct
re- red-	re-	1. back, in return 2. again	redirect
sub- suc- suf- sug- sum- sup- sur- sus-	sub-	under, below, beneath, secondary	suprapubic
syl- sym- syn- sys-	syn-	together similar	symbiotic

Do NOT double the consonants in the following words

- in short words which end in 'x'

e.g   box   boxes

- in words of foreign origin e.g. words ending in –et

e.g. sachet, tourniquet

- in simple words which end in more than one consonant – it already has a double consonant

-nk	-lt	-mp	-nt
tank	felt	lump	went

- after words which end in with 'ck' – these are considered to be double consonants

truck   lucky   sucked

- after words which end in –tch -these are considered to be double consonants

batch   watch   latch

- before suffixes

ment	some	ry
ailment	chromosome	ambulatory
commitment	cumbersome	auditory
compartment	irksome	capillary
development	meddlesome	exemplary
discouragement	quarrelsome	injury
document	tiresome	satisfactory
instrument		

Rules for words with 'l'

Note: These rules apply to British English. There is no doubling of 'l' in U.S English in these words.

- If the base word has a **short vowel**, double the 'l' before adding a suffix which begins with a vowel or semivowel 'y'

- If the base word has a **long vowel,** do not double the 'l' when adding a suffix which begins with a vowel or semivowel 'y'

- Exception to the rule: *parallel*

- Do not double the 'l' in words which end in –alist

- Do not double the final 'l' in words which end in -ful or –fil

Base word	+full or +fill	Term
beauty	full	beautiful
deceit	full	deceitful
doubt	full	doubtful
duty	full	dutiful
full	fill	fulfil, fulfilment
mouth	full	mouthful
pain	full	painful
peace	full	peaceful
skill	full	skilful
spoon	full	spoonful
will	full	wilful

Base word	suffix	Term (Brit Eng)	Term (US Eng)
appeal	-ing	appealing	appealing
cancel	-ation	cancellation	cancelation
cancel	-ed	cancelled	canceled
final	-ist	finalist	finalist
fool	-ish	foolish	foolish
ideal	-ist	idealist	idealist
instrumental	-ist	instrumentalist	instrumentalist
parallel	-ogram	**parallelogram**	**parallelogram**
		unparalleled	**unparalleled**
propel	-ant	propellant	propellant
travel	-er	traveller	traveler
jewel	-ery	jewellery	jewelry
rebel	-ious	rebellious	rebelious

• before words which end in the following. **Words in bold have a double 'll'**

-ic	-ical	-id	-it	-ish	-ule
academic	anatomical	acid	audit	abolish	ampoule
acidic	botanical	insipid	benefit	blemish	capsule
alcoholic	economical	**pallid**	biscuit	diminish	cellule
athletic	historical	rapid	circuit	embellish	ferrule
chronic	tropical	solid	conduit	famish	globule
clinic		squalid	culprit	finish	granule
colic		tepid	decrepit	replenish	joule
conic		torrid	deficit	tarnish	lobule
dynamic		turbid	exhibit	vanish	molecule
epidemic		valid	gambit		nebule
eugenic			inhibit		pustule
euphoric			limit		reschedule
genetic			prohibit		rule
ironic					schedule
metallic					
myopic					
organic					
panic					
paralytic					
phallic					
static					

Words with 's'

• There is equal preference for doubling or not doubling the 's' when adding a suffix which begins with a vowel or semivowel 'y' . Some preferences prevail.

Base Word	Suffix	Term
bonus	-es	bonuses
focus	-ing	focussing or focusing
nonplus	-ed	nonplussed
pus	-y	pussy

Words with 'r' and 't'

• Do not double final 'r' or 't' before a suffix beginning with a vowel **when the stress falls on the first syllable of the base-word** e.g. differ → difference

• Do not double the final consonant **when the stress falls on the first syllable of the base-word after a suffix has been added to it** e.g. prefer (stress on last syllable) → preference (stress on last syllable after suffix added)

• Double the final consonant before a suffix beginning with a vowel **when the stress falls on the last syllable of the base-word:** e.g. prefer → preference

Base word in	suffix	New Term -rr-	New Term -r-
aver	-ed	averred	
blur	-ed	blurred	
blur	-y	blurry	
career	-ed		careered
concur	-ed	concurred	
concur	-ence	concurrence	
confer	-ed	conferred	
confer	-ence		conference
defer	-ed	deferred	
defer	-ence		deference
deter	-al	deferral	
deter	-ant	deterrent	
differ	-ent		different
differ	-ence		difference
differ	-ed		differed
fur	-y	furry	
incur	-ed	incurred	
infer	-ed	inferred	
infer	-ence		inference
interfere	-ed		interfered
interfere	-ence		interference
inter	-ed	interred	
inter	-ment		interment
jeer	-ed		jeered

leer	-ed		leered
occur	-ed	occurred	
occur	-ence	occurrence	
orienteer	-ing		orienteering
peer	-ed		peered
persevere	-ed		persevered
persevere	-ance		perseverance
prefer	-ed	preferred	
prefer	-ence		preference
prefer	-ential		preferential
proffer	-ed		proffered
recur	-ed		
recur	-ence	recurrence	
reengineer	-ed		reengineered
refer	-al	referral	
refer	-ence		reference
sever	-ed		severed
sever	-ance		severance
slur	-ed	slurred	
suffer	-ed		suffered
suffer	-ance		sufferance
transfer	-ed	transferred	
transfer	-ence		transference
veer	-ed		veered
volunteer	-ed		volunteered

How To Tackle Medical Terms

The words you come across when studying Anatomy and Physiology may have their origin in

Old English

Everyday words which describe body parts

head	nose	shoulder	body	blood
brain	nostril	arm	belly	bone
hair	mouth	elbow	navel	marrow
lock of hair	tongue	hand	liver	sinew
forehead	tooth	wrist	gut	gall
brow	lip	palm	bladder	skin
cheek	ear	thumb	bosom	
chin	eye	hip	breast	
beard	eyelid	thigh	heart	
neck		knee	rib	
throat		limb	breastbone	
		shank	chest	
		toe	lung	

Greek

The Greeks were the first anatomists so it is reasonable that we have their legacy in words relating to the human body and some words which describe diseases e.g nephritis. Nephritis = inflammation of the kidney and comes from nephr- the word part which means kidney.

Latin

The Romans conquered the Greeks and took advantage of the Greeks' advanced knowledge of the human body. They studied from Greek slave doctors and then used some of their own words to describe anatomy and disease processes. For example, renal disease = kidney disease comes from ren- (the Latin word part which means kidney)

Eponyms

Eponyms come from epi- which means after in this case and -nym which means name. This is the use of the name of the discoverer of a particular body part or anatomy of disease e.g. the Loop of Henle.

Common Medical Eponyms

Eponym	Meaning
Addison's Disease	adrenal insufficiency
Alzheimer's Disease	type of dementia
Apgar Score	score of the health of a newborn
Asperger's Syndrome	impaired ability to relate to people socially
Babinski sign	extension of the toe upwards when the sole of the foot is stroked - an abnormal neurological response
Baker's cyst	cyst on the knee
Barrett's Oesophagus	narrowing of the oesophagus
Bartholin gland	small glands near the vaginal opening
Beau's lines	lines across the nail plate which develop during high stress to the body
Bell's palsy	nerve palsy which affects one side of the face
Bence Jones proteins	type of immunoglobulin found in blood disorders
Bowen's capsule	covering of the glomerulus in the kidney
Braxton-Hicks contractions	painless contractions during the late stages of pregnancy
Chadwick's sign	blue-red colouring of the cervix from the 7th week of pregnancy
Cheyne-Stokes breathing	breathing pattern abnormality often seen in the last stages of life
Chvostek's (say 'Vostek') sign	test for low calcium in tetany by tapping the facial nerve in front of the ear
Colles' fracture	fracture of the wrist
Coombs test	blood test used to test for haemolytic anaemia
Cowpers Gland	small glands below the prostate
Creutzfeld-Jakob Disease CJD	rare degenerative neurological disease

Eponym	Meaning
Crohn's Disease	type of gastrointestinal tract inflammation
Cushing's Disease	excess production of cortisol
Down Syndrome	congenital disease causing developmental delay
Duchenne's muscular dystrophy	progressive degeneration of the muscles of the body
Dupuytren's syndrome	fibromatosis of the palm of the hand
Epstein-Barr virus	cause of glandular fever
Eustachian tube	canal in the middle ear
Ewing's sarcoma	type of bone cancer
Tetralogy of Fallot	heart disorder which includes a ventricular septal defect
Gilbert's syndrome	condition of excess bilirubin in the blood and jaundice
Goodell's sign	softening of the cervix around the 8th week of pregnancy
Graafian follicle	fluid-filled sac which develops in the ovary
Graves' Disease	excess thyroid which causes the development of goitre
Guillain-Barré syndrome	kind of nerve disease which affects nervous function
Guthrie test	test for PKU (phenylketonuria) in babies
Hansen's Disease	leprosy
Hashimoto's encephalopathy	complications of thyroid disease which mimic stroke or dementia
Hegar's sign	softening of the uterus during the first trimester of pregnancy
Heimlich manoeuvre	abdominal thrust used in choking
Loop of Henle	one of the sections of the nephron in the kidney

Eponym	Meaning
Hippocratic oath	the doctor's oath to do no harm to their patients
Hirschprung's Disease	congenital disease of the large intestine
Hodgkin's disease	type of lymphoma
Holter monitor	continuous ambulatory ECG monitoring
Homan's sign	pain and tenderness of the calf in the presence of a DVT
Huntington's disease	progressive jerky movements and severe dementia
Ishihara plates	plates with coloured dots in different patterns to test for colour blindness
Islets of Langerhans	insulin-producing cells in the pancreas
Kaposi's sarcoma	type of skin cancer seen in AIDS
Kawasaki's disease	acute febrile illness seen in children
Kegel exercises	exercises used to prevent urinary incontinence
Klinefelter syndrome	chromosome abnormality
Koch's bacillus	TB bacillus
Koplik's spots	white spots on the inside of the cheeks which are seen in measles
Korotkoff sounds	sounds between systolic and diastolic blood pressure readings
Korsakoff's syndrome	memory loss seen in alcoholism
Kupffer cells	cells found in the liver
Kussmaul's breathing	over-breathing seen in diabetic ketoacidosis DKA
Laennec's cirrhosis	in alcoholic cirrhosis, nodules found on the surface of the liver
Legionnaire's disease	pneumonia often caused through faulty air conditioning
Lewy body dementia	dementia associated with Parkinson's disease

Eponym	Meaning
Leydig cell tumour	testicular tumour
Lou Gehrig's Disease	amyotrophic lateral sclerosis ALS, progressive degenerative disease
Lyme disease	inflammatory disease spread by a tick
Mallory-Weiss tears	small tears in the oesophagus after violent retching
Mantoux test	TB test under the skin
Marfan's syndrome	chromosomal disorder which often leads to enlargement of the aorta
Mee's lines	white lines on the nails often seen in arsenic poisoning
Meissner's corpuscle	receptors in the skin which respond to light touch
Ménière's disease	disorder of the vestibular area of the ear resulting in vertigo
Möbius sign	eye abnormality in thyroid disease
Montgomery glands	glands around the areola of the breast
Morton's neuroma	painful nerve tumour found between the toes
Munchausen's syndrome	psychiatric disorder where the sufferer invents symptoms of diseases to attract attention
Sphincter of Oddi	sphincter around the opening of the common bile duct
Paget's disease	chronic bone disorder which causes deformity of the bones
Pap smear	test for cancer of the cervix
Parkinson's Disease	degenerative disease causing a rigid gait and dementia
Perthes test	test for hip dysplasia or 'clicky hips'
Pott's fracture	fracture of the fibula
Prader-Willi Syndrome	chromosomal disorder resulting in insatiable appetite

Eponym	Meaning

Eponym	Meaning
Prinzmetal's angina	variant angina which occurs in rest
Raynaud's syndrome	vascular disorder with excessive reaction to the cold
Schick's test	test for diphtheria
Sjögren's syndrome	disease which causes dry mouth and dry eyes
Smith's fracture	fracture of the distal radius from a fall onto the back of the hand
Stokes-Adams attacks	syncope or fainting with heart block involvement
Tay-Sachs disease	hereditary enzyme deficiency leading to developmental delay
Tourette's syndrome	neurological disorder which leads to unwanted uttering of words or obscenities out of context
Trendelenburg's position	patient position before an operation where the body lies flat with both feet elevated
Turner's syndrome	chromosome abnormality which leads to physical and reproductive system abnormalities
Usher's syndrome	rare genetic disorder which leads to deaf-blindness
Valsalva manoeuvre	forceful breathing out against a closed airway by closing the mouth and pinching the nose
ampulla of Vater	sphincter around the opening of the common bile duct
Volkmann contraction	permanent contraction of the hand so that it looks claw-like
von Willebrand disease	cause of haemophilia

Eponym	Meaning

The Apostrophe

Apostrophes were first used around the time that printing presses came into use. Previously, the only manuscripts which could be produced were copied one by one.

Punctuation marks were used to show the reader where to breathe and how long to pause. Symbols such as the hedera or ivy leaf separated words in the way hyphens are used now. Ivy leaves were very decorative and became part of the art-work of the page.

Early printers started using an apostrophe to show that a letter or several letters were missing from a word. Common examples:

o'clock   means 'of the clock'

can't   means 'cannot'

it's   means 'it is'

Around the 17th and 18th centuries the apostrophe began to be used before plural endings especially if the noun was a foreign borrowing ending in a vowel. It wasn't until after the 18th century that the apostrophe started to be used to indicate possession.

The rules for using apostrophes

Rule	Example
Write apostrophe s ('s) after a single noun	John's book means 'the book of John'
Write apostrophe s ('s) after names which end in -s if the 's' is pronounced	Mr Jones's book means 'the book of Mr Jones'
Write apostrophe only (') after names which end in -s if the 's' is not pronounced	Bridges'
Use apostrophe s ('s) after the second name only if two people possess the same item.	Bill and Judy's house
Write apostrophe only (') after ancient names e.g. Socrates	Socrates' ideas means ' the ideas of Socrates'
Write apostrophe only (') after Moses	Moses' Ten Commandments means 'Ten Commandments of Moses'
Expressions of time	two weeks' time
No apostrophe with the plurals of capital letters and numbers used as nouns	In the 50s 1990s
Write apostrophe s ('s) with 'one'	one's house
Write no apostrophe with 'her'	The book is hers

Rule	Example
Use apostrophe s ('s) in some expressions	no if's and but's I've dotted the i's and crossed the t's.
Use apostrophe s ('s) when talking about letters in the alphabet	How many l's are there in the word 'apple'?
Write s apostrophe (s') after plural nouns	the girls' dresses
Write apostrophe s ('s) in irregular plural nouns	children's, women's
The Double Possessive Write apostrophe s ('s) if you are referring to a living object e.g. a person	*Bill, a friend of my sister's, showed me the book.*
The Double Possessive Write no apostrophe if you are referring to a object e.g. a thing	*I'm a fan of the Oxford Dictionary (not Dictionary's)*
No apostrophe with possessive pronoun	his, hers, its, theirs ours yours whose.

Compound Words and Collocations

Currently, around 40% of new words entering the English language enter as compound words. Compound words are combinations of two or more separate words which express a single idea.

They can be formed by combining nouns, verbs, adjectives or adverbs. As compound words they function as nouns, verbs, adjectives or adverbs. Compound words are very common in Medical English as many of the terms are new or describe new concepts. Many compounds are collocations because they are only found in a particular form.

Compound words are divided into three types or forms:

open,

closed

hyphenated .

Sometimes it isn't easy to decide which form to use but the following is a guide:

(1) **Open** (or spaced) compound words
 are either easily understood and accepted as two or more separate words or they are compounds in the early stages of entry into the language.

Open compounds – noun compounds	Example
Proper nouns denoting race, place of residence or origin	New Yorker Swiss German
names of methods, functions or procedures	birth control bed rest blood pressure dipstick
names of diseases or conditions	haemolytic anaemia stomach ache back ache tooth ache period pain flare up check up follow up congestive cardiac failure
single eponyms + test or disease	Coombs test
colours where the first colour acts as an adjective	reddish brown jet black (hair)
Do not use a hyphen with these suffixes -less -long -out, -over -wide -wise	clueless yearlong walkout carryover worldwide clockwise

(2) **Hyphenated** compound words: are usually in the transition period from open to closed compound words. The trend is to avoid hyphens in forming compounds and hyphenated compounds are more common in British English than American English.

Use a hyphen	Example
two or more eponyms to describe one disease or disorder	Henle-Lexer-Coenen sign
when the base word has a capital letter or is an acronym	pro-Stalinist pre-AIDS
compound adjectives with a preposition but only before a noun. Otherwise without a hyphen	up-to-date information. She is up to date with the information a down-to-earth person. on-the-job training. He was trained on the job. end-to-end anastomosis small-to-medium moderate-to-large matter-of-fact sleight-of-hand **Not usually with foreign expressions:** café au lait (spots)
adjectives with participles Present Participle ends in – ing Past Participle ends in -ed (regular) -en, -n –t (irreg)	high-ranking long-standing (illness) odd-sounding (name) ready-made (meals) smooth-talking (salesman) sweet-smelling (flowers) foul-smelling (breath)

nouns with participles before a noun	awe-inspiring (stories) face-saving (interventions) law-abiding (citizen) smoke-filled (flat) eye-catching (design) bed-wetting
noun and an adjective is **always hyphenated**	age-old (problem) brain-dead sky-high (costs) water-repellent (dressings) HIV-positive gram-negative diet-controlled (diabetes) labour-saving patient-centred eye-opener
adjective and noun compound before a noun	broad-minded quick-witted hot-tempered middle-aged old-fashioned low-grade high-risk over-worked over-wrought same-sex short-term under-nourished well-hydrated
a compound nouns of titles or names e.g	Italian-American (descent) chief-of-staff
two nouns of equal value or importance which join together to form one noun	clerk-typist cardioversion- defibrillator obsessive-compulsive father-son (relationship) nurse-patient (trust)

numbers in a compound before a noun which form a single idea	four-year-old child one-litre bag (of IV fluids) 5 cm-wide wound one-week course but a one week's course a 6 - day history of low back pain six- to seven-day course of treatment **Not with percentages:** a 3% rise
Fractions as adjectives	two-fifths of the population **Not when used as a noun** twenty-two hundredths
with dates	mid-March post-1989
with ratios	I-to-E ratio BUN-Creatinine ratio
when need for clarity	re-use rather than reuse
adjectives joined by 'and'	cut-and-dried hard-and-fast (rule) up-and-coming (specialist) high-and-mighty (attitude) on-and-off rough-and-tumble (play of children) tried-and-tested (method) spic-and-span (clinic) open-and-shut (case)

two adjectives which represent two sides of something	true-false questions
colour adjectives	blue-black snow-white green-grey (green-gray US) red-topped jar purple-lidded tube
with the suffix 'self'	self-esteem self-evident self-examination self-referred
with the suffix 'free'	paraben-free seizure-free preservative-free
with the suffix -like when the stem word ends in 'l' or is a proper noun. Otherwise, do not use a hyphen	ball-like Ebola-like But: childlike
with the prefix 'non'	non-Hodgkin's lymphoma non-insulin-dependent-diabetes non-weight bearing
when the letter which ends the first word is the same as the letter which starts the second word – to make pronunciation clearer	meta-analysis co-operation

(3) **Closed** (or solid) compound words:

are compound words in the final stage of acceptance into common usage. Familiarity with the compound word allows it to be spelled as one word.

Closed compounds	Example
These prefixes form closed compounds	ante antecedent anti anticoagulant bi biphasic co coefficient contra contraceptive counter counterproductive de extra infra inter interrelated micro microscope mid over overuse pseudo semi semicircular super trans transfer tri triangular
measurement	teaspoonful fingerbreadth
names of family members	grandparent grandchild **But:** great-grandchild
With the suffixes -maker or -making	policymaker troublemaker **But:** decision-making

Common Collocations

cerebrovascular accident	stroke
fatal accident	accident which ends in a death
accident-prone	someone who keeps having accidents
back ache	pain felt in the back
bellyache	pain felt in the abdomen
ear ache	pain felt in the ear
headache	pain felt in the head, cephalagia
muscle ache	pain felt in the muscle
stomach ache	pain felt in the abdomen, gastritis
toothache	pain felt in the tooth
alcohol addiction	physical and emotional need for alcohol
caffeine addiction	physical and emotional need for coffee
drug addiction	physical and emotional need for any drug
nicotine addiction	physical and emotional need for tobacco
opiate addiction	physical and emotional need for morphine-like drugs
anxiety attack	severe anxiousness
attack of nerves	severe nervousness
attack of hysteria	severe nervousness
heart attack	myocardial infarction
suicide attempt	trying to kill oneself
blood bank	laboratory where blood stores are kept
blood cell	single unit which makes up the components of blood
blood clot	thrombus
blood count	counting of white blood cells, red cells and platelets
blood disease	haematological disease
blood disorder	haematological disorder
blood dyscrasia	any abnormal condition of the blood
blood group	also called blood type. grouping of blood based on the

	presence of certain antigens
blood line	descendants of a person, blood relatives
blood pressure	pressure of blood against the artery walls
bloodshed	slaughter of people
bloodstained	contaminated with blood
bloodstream	flow of blood through the blood vessels
blood test	drawing a sample of blood for testing
blood transfusion	IV infusion of blood products
blood type	see blood group
blood vessel	tubes in the body which carry blood
cord blood	blood which flows in the umbilical cord to a baby
menstrual blood	blood lost during a period (menstruation)
whole blood	blood which contains all components
body fluids	any of the fluids excreted by the body e.g. urine, sweat
body mass index	measurement of the percentage of fat and muscle in the body by multiplying height times weight
bedbug	insects which living in bedding and feed on human blood
flu bug	everyday expression for influenza
stomach bug	everyday expression for gastroenteritis
travel bug	(1) desire to travel (2) a travel bug – infection when travelling, usually diarrhoea and vomiting
bedsore	Now called Pressure Ulcer
dementia care	specific care for patients who have dementia
palliative care	specific care for patients who have a terminal illness which is no longer able to be cured or treated
drug dependence	a psychological or physiological need for a drug
oxygen dependence	clinical need for oxygen
coughing fit	continuous coughing which cannot be stopped
epileptic fit	attack of epilepsy where the sufferer often loses consciousness for a short time
fit of giggling	continuous giggling which cannot be stopped
sneezing fit	continuous sneezing which cannot be stopped

heart failure	stopping of normal heart function
kidney failure	stopping of normal kidney function
organ failure	stopping of normal function of the body's major organs
febrile convulsions	fits brought on by continued very high temperatures
hay fever	sneezing and sinusitis caused by allergies
fever blister	cold sores
fluid balance	equal balance between fluids going in and out of the body
fluid balance chart	recording or all fluid going in and out of the body
fluid intake	any fluid which a person drinks or has administered through a drip or tube feed
IV fluid	any fluid which is giving through a vein or into the subcutaneous layer of skin
fluid loss	any fluid which is excreted from the body
fluid output	the amount of fluid which is excreted from the body
health information	information about healthy living or the treatment of diseases
health literacy	the knowledge of health issues especially relating to your own health needs
mental health	psychological well-being
health problem	any disease ,disorder or condition which affects a person
heart attack	myocardial infarction, the sudden stopping of the heart
heart disease	any disease which affects the healthy functioning of the heart
heart failure	stopping of normal functioning of the heart
adverse incident	unexpected and unwanted event which causes injury
incident report	report which is made after an adverse incident or near miss to alert authorities of the occurrence
cross infection	taking infective agents from one area or person to another
hospital acquired infection	infections which are acquired as a result of

infection control	hospitalisation
	measures which aim to reduce infections
nosocomial infection	the older term for hospital acquired infection
opportunistic infection	infection which affects a person who is already debilitated by another infection
kidney disease	any disease which affects the healthy functioning of the kidneys
kidney failure	also called renal failure. May be divided into Acute Renal Failure or Chronic Kidney Disease (CKD) ,also called CRF (Chronic Renal Failure)
manual dexterity	ability to use your hands well e.g to pick up an object
manual handling	now also called Moving and Handling. The moving and handling of people and objects in a way which avoids injury
medical management	treatment of a case using medication rather than surgery
surgical management	treatment of a case using surgical procedures
wound management	treatment of wounds using appropriate cleansing solutions and dressings
muscle contraction	tensing of muscles by shortening the muscle fibres
muscle spasm	sudden gripping sensation in a muscle
muscle strength	the measurement of how strong a muscle is
muscle tone	elasticity of muscles
pelvic floor muscle	the muscles in the perineum
catheter pack	a sterile pack with all the equipment needed to catheterise a patient
dressing pack	a sterile pack with all the equipment needed to dress a wound
acute pain	sharp, short-term pain
back pain	pain felt often in the lower back
chronic pain	long-term pain often aching rather than sharp pain
pain relief	painkillers
pain control	measures which reduce pain to a bearable level
pain management	the use of as many means as possible to reduce pain
painful stimuli	something which causes a person to feel pain

inpatient	a patient who has been admitted to hospital
outpatient	a patient who attends a hospital clinic without staying in hospital
patient confidentiality	keeping any personal information secure and not disclosing it to unauthorised people
patient controlled analgesia	PCA. a method of pain control delivered as IV fluids which patient access by pressing on a button
patient rights	a list of events which patients can expect to happen whilst in hospital e.g right to safe treatment
patient responsibilities	the responsibility of patients to perform certain tasks e.g. accept medical treatment when offered
carbon monoxide poisoning	toxic reaction to the gas carbon monoxide
food poisoning	toxic reaction to a micro-organism in contaminated food. also called *gastroenteritis*
lead poisoning	toxic reaction to the lead. Also called *saturnism*
mercury poisoning	toxic reaction to mercury
pressure area	area in the body which is subjected to more pressure than normal e.g. by sitting for long periods
pressure bandage	type of firm bandaging used to stop excessive bleeding
blood pressure	see above
pressure dressing	a dressing often used with a pressure bandage to stop excessive bleeding
intraocular pressure	IOP, pressure levels in the eye ball
peer pressure	psychological pressure exerted on people in a particular group
pressure-relieving mattress	an air-filled mattress which minimises pressure on the body, used on bed-ridden patients
flow rate	the speed at which a liquid flows
pulse rate	the speed of the pulse; heart rate
respiratory rate	the speed of breathing in and out
self awareness	understanding of your characteristics or traits
self-centred	only concerned with yourself
self-conscious	shy

self-control	ability to behave in a restrained manner
self-discipline	a synonym of *self-control*
self-esteem	feeling of your own value
self medicate	patients who give themselves their own medication whilst in hospital
air sickness	type of motion sickness especially during bumpy plane trips
altitude sickness	also called *mountain sickness*; symptoms of oxygen deficiency
car sickness	motion sickness experienced during a car journey
morning sickness	sickness which is often experienced during the morning when pregnant. *Hyperemesis gravidarum* is the term for severe vomiting during pregnancy
motion sickness	sickness experienced during any movement
sea sickness	sickness experienced during changing movement on a boat
sleeping sickness	type of sickness which makes suffers extremely sleepy
sterile field	sterile area which is produced around a wound or surgical site
sterile scissors	scissors which have been autoclaved to remove bacteria
sterile supply	department in a hospital which sterilises re-usable equipment and surgical supplies
stomach ache	pain felt in the abdomen
upset stomach	everyday expression for gastroenteritis
stress fracture	a fracture which is caused by heavy loads being repeatedly placed on a bone
stress incontinence	involuntary incontinence caused by sneezing, coughing or lifting heavy objects
stress-induced	something which is brought on by stress
stress test	a test which measures the effect of stress on a body organ e.g. the heart
anticoagulant therapy	drug therapy used to prevent blood clotting
drug therapy	medications

hypnotherapy	therapy using hypnosis
IV therapy	use of intravenous fluids
physiotherapy	use of physical manipulation and exercise
psychotherapy	use of psychological support
radiotherapy	use of radiation to treat diseases especially cancer
strep throat	throat infection caused by a streptococcal infection
throat infection	pharyngitis
tooth abscess	infection in or around the tooth
toothache	pain in a tooth
tooth alignment	the correct lining up of teeth
tooth brush	implement used to clean teeth
tooth decay	infection in teeth, called *dental caries*
tooth extraction	removal of a tooth
toothpaste	soft material used on a toothbrush to clean teeth
alcohol withdrawal	stopping the intake of alcohol
drug withdrawal	stopping the use of drugs
withdrawal method	form of contraception where the penis is removed from the vagina before ejaculation
withdrawal symptoms	unpleasant sensations experienced when stopping the intake of a drug or alcohol

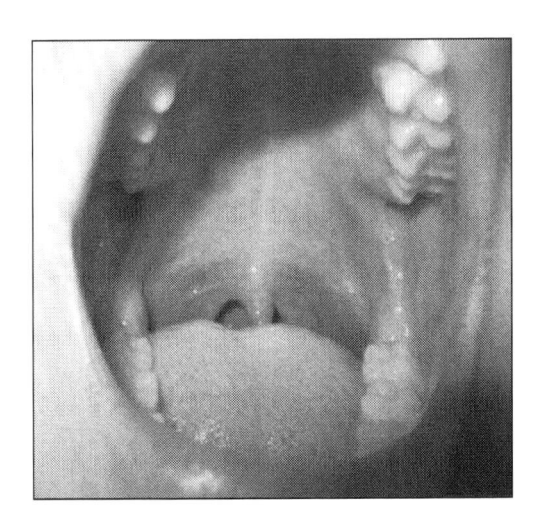

Plurals

Plurals are divided into the following:

Regular plurals

- add -es or -s to the end of a noun

Letter	Single Noun	+ s or + es	Plural Noun
c	space	s	spaces
ch	torch	es	torches
sh	wash	es	washes
s	loss	es	losses
z	graze	s	grazes
all consonants	wounds	s	wounds

Nouns only found in the plural Form

Plural Noun	Examples		
Binary: Names of instruments or medical equipment with two parts	forceps tweezers clippers	pliers nasal cannulae	scissors callipers
Binary: Types of glasses	binoculars spectacles	glasses	goggles
Binary: clothing	jeans pants gloves	leggings trousers scrubs	overalls shorts
Aggregate Nouns : nouns made up of many parts	data faeces hiccups remains	dregs fauces liquids scabies	eardrops herpes pubes tonsils
Names of subject areas	linguistics mathematics physics		
Names of diseases	measles mumps scabies	rabies shingles	

Irregular plurals

Final vowel - single form	plural form	Plural form	Plural form
-a	-ae	-as	-ata
agenda		agendas	
alga	algae		
amoeba	amoebae	amoebas	
corona	coronae	coronas	
fistula		fistulas	
formula	formulae	formulas	
hyperbola		hyperbolas	
lamina	laminae	laminas	
maxilla	maxillae		
melanoma		melanomas	
persona	personae		
placenta		placentas	
quota		quotas	
scapula		scapulas	
stigma			stigmata
stoma			stomata
vesica	vesicae		
vista		vistas	

- o	- os	-oes	
aficionado	aficionados		
albino	albinos		
hero		heroes	
innuendo	innuendos	innuendoes	
libido	libidos		
memo	memos		
placebo	placebos		
ratio	ratios		
zero	zeros		
-us	**- i**	**-uses**	
alumnus	alumni		
apparatus			
bacillus	bacilli		
callus		calluses	
campus		campuses	
focus		focuses	
fungus	fungi		
genius	genii	geniuses	
hiatus		hiatuses	
humerus		humeruses	
malleus			
radius	radii		
- o	- os	-oes	

-um	-a	-ums	
addendum	addenda		
bacterium	bacteria		
cerebellum	cerebella		
cerebrum	cerebra		
conundrum		conundrums	
curriculum	curricula	curriculums	
datum	data		
delerium		deleriums	
dictum	dicta	dictums	
erratum	errata		
memorandum	memoranda		
millenium	millennia		
museum		museums	
ovum	ova		
proscenium	proscenia		
pterygium	pterygia	pterygiums	
quorum		quorums	
referendum	referenda	referendums	
serum	sera	serums	
stratum	strata	stratums	
symposium	symposia		
trapezium	trapezia	trapeziums	
-um	-a	-ums	

-eau	-eaux	-eaus	
bureau	bureaux	bureaus	
plateau	plateaus	plateaux	
-is	**-es**		
analysis	analyses		
antithesis	antitheses		
basis	bases		
crisis	crises		
diagnosis	diagnoses		
emphasis	emphases		
hypothesis	hypotheses		
neurosis	neuroses		
oasis	oases		
parenthesis	parentheses		
psychosis	psychoses		
synopsis	synopses		
thesis	theses		
-f -ife	**-fs**	**-ves -ives**	
belief	beliefs		
dwarf		dwarves	
half		halves	
motif	motifs		
proof	proofs		
self		selves	
midwife	midwives		

2. Irregular plurals which change the form of the single noun.

singular	plural form 'foreign form'	plural form 'English form'
apex	apices	apexes
aphid	aphides	
appendix	appendices	appendixes
auspice	auspices	
bus	buses	busses
cervix	cervices	cervixes
cicatrice	cicatrices	
coccyx	coccyges	
corpus	corpora	corpuses
criterion	criteria	
die	dice	
genus	genera	
index	indices	indexes
insignia	insignia	insignias
lumen	lumens	lumina
matrix	matrices	matrixes
opus	opera	
lumen	lumens	lumina
phenomenon	phenomena	
vortex	vortices	vortexes

3. Irregular plurals with two forms which have two different meanings

singular	plural meaning (1)	plural meaning (2)
antenna	antennas metal apparatus for receiving electronic signals	antennae sensory appendage on insects
appendix	appendixes accepted form for body organ and end matter of a book	appendices traditional form
medium	media type of publication e.g TV, ebook	mediums

4. Irregular plurals which are irregular because they retain the single noun form.

singular	plural
corps	corps
crossroads	crossroads
means	means
offspring	offspring
series	series
species	species

5. Irregular plurals which have a completely different plurals from the singular.

singular	irregular plural
brother	brethren
child	children
foot	feet
louse	lice
man	men
person	people
tooth	teeth
woman	women

6. Irregular plurals of compound nouns

singular of compound words	plural of compound words
also-ran	also-rans
attorney-general	attorneys-general
commander-in-chief	commanders-in-chief
court-martial	courts-martial
editor-in-chief	editors-in-chief
ex-husband	ex-husbands
ex-wife	ex-wives
go-between	go-betweens
listener-in	listeners-in
mother-in-law	mothers-in-law
passer-by	passers-by

Uncountable nouns

Uncount Noun	examples
Mass	liquids water coffee tea chemicals metals gases oxygen carbon dioxide ozone
Collective nouns	Equipment furniture medical devices Knowledge information documentation Research data Advice
Abstract Nouns	**Often end in :** **-ance/-ence** performance **-ity** capacity commodity **-tion** satisfaction distribution friction **-ism** dwarfism **-abilty** ability **-ship** friendship **-ness** stiffness **-cy** lunacy efficiency **-ment** assessment **-age** age adage roughage foliage **-hood** childhood

Uncount Noun	examples
Field of study Note: some are plural nouns but are thought of as single	science – nanotechnology pathology medicine nursing mathematics physics mechanics acoustics ethics
Processes and actions	Suffixes often end in -ing imaging recycling monitoring -tion production evaporation
diseases and medical conditions Note: some diseases have a plural form but are treated as a single noun	heart disease whooping cough tuberculosis pneumonia measles scabies shingles mumps rickets rabies

Uncount Noun	examples

Definite and indefinite articles

Use the definite article 'the' with	
Singular species	The dolphin is an endangered species
Singular inventions	He invented the telephone
Name of rivers, seas, oceans, mountain regions, deserts	The Pacific Ocean The Yangtze River The North Sea The Sahara Desert The Midlands
Names of places with 'of'	The Tower of London, The University of Bath
Names of museums, theatres, hotels	The British Museum The Lyric Theatre The Ritz
When it is clear there is only one person or thing	That must be the postman
Superlatives	That is the best cake I have ever eaten
Some time expressions	In the morning in the evening in the night (meaning 'at some time during the night) But: at night (at a particular time during the night)
A unique object, person or group of people	The Earth is round, The Beatles are famous, the Dalai Lama
A noun when it is mentioned a second time	He stole a car. The car was badly damaged
When you mean something particular	The book you want is at the bookshop now
Names of highways	The M1
Names of newspapers	The Courier Mail

Use the indefinite article 'a' or 'an' with	
For general meaning (any)	Give me an apple .
	Implied 'It doesn't matter which apple'
When you mean a general type of something	I've never had a pet turtle
With a noun mentioned the first time	There was a dog in the garden. The dog barked at me.
	'A dog' refers to 'any dog' , 'the dog' is 'the dog I mentioned before, i.e a particular dog'
With numbers and fractions	one hundred and fifty, a half
	But: U.S form 'one hundred fifty'
To describe a job or profession or to describe characteristics	She's a doctor
	She's a caring nurse
With abstract uncount nouns + adjective – way of counting uncouncount nouns	She has a passionate hatred of snakes
	'hatred' is an uncount noun which would not normally take an indefinite article e.g Hatred is a destructive emotion

Use no article (zero article) with	
With the names of : towns cities countries	China is a large country Brisbane is a city on a river Chile **But: Some countries are referred to using 'the'** The United Kingdom, The United States of America, The United Arab Emirates The Ukraine
When speaking generally about plurals	Dolphins are wonderful creatures
When speaking generally about uncount nouns	Diabetes is a serious problem around the world
With names of meals	lunch breakfast
With airports, stations, schools or colleges	Brisbane Airport, City Station, Newtown College
Roads, streets	Bundall Road
With festivals	Christmas, New Year, Ramadan

Use of Capital letters

When to use a capital letter	Example
First word (any word) of a sentence	Few people have ever heard of gfhsluf.
Names of: days of the week months of the year **But not:** names of seasons	Sunday, Monday, Tuesday, Wednesday, Thursday, Friday, Saturday, Wednesdays February spring summer autumn fall winter
Names of languages	French Italian
Words connected to a particular place **But not:** if part of a fixed phrase	Mancunian (from Manchester) Sydney-sider cornish pasty
Words which identify nationalities or ethnic groups **Note:** Former ethnic labels which are considered offensive should not be used	Inuits Bosnian **Acceptable labels:** native American native Australian Black American (capital 'b' and 'a')
Proper names : names of people, places and things **Note:** some foreign names include words like *van der, von, de ,bin* to indicate belonging to a family or aristocratic group. Do not capitalise these words unless accepted practice	Virginia van der Water Professor Jim Smith Saint Paul (but *patron saint* of) Winter Olympics
Referring to a particular institution	The English Parliament The Australian Government
Geographic regions with a distinct identity	The Middle East Southeast Asia South Africa
Names of historical periods	the Middle Ages, the Cold War
Names of religious terms (religions, religious festivals)	Christmas, Ramadan, Hanukkah Islam, Christianity, Hinduism God, the Prophet

When to use a capital letter	Example
Policy 1: In titles of books, poems, films etc the first word and every significant word Policy 2: Capital letter in the first letter only unless there is an independent reason for using a capital letter (e.g. the word 'God' to distinguish from (a) 'god'	*Cambridge English for Nursing* this is the form used *Cambridge English for nursing* this would be the form used under policy 2
The first word of a direct quotation which is a complete sentence. Not used when quoting a word or several words only	Allum stated that 'Nursing Assistants report any changes in patient condition to the RN within the team.' Allum stated that any alteration in timing of assessments or 'patient condition' should always be passed on.
Brand names	Band Aids , Kleenex. Some brand names have become part of general usage and are assumed to refer to any similar product so may be found without a capital letter e.g Kleenex
Roman Numerals But not in the apothecary system	Henry IV LIV equals fifty-four
The pronoun 'I'	I am sure that I have already spoken about this.
Used as emphasis **But:** do not use in emails as it is construed as 'shouting'	I AM SICK OF YOUR POINTLESS COMMENTS.

Writing Numbers

Number	in words	Prefix
0.1	zero point one	deci-
0.01	zero point zero one	
0.001	zero point zero zero one	
1/10	one tenth	
2/10	two tenths	
1/100	one hundredth	
1/1000	one thousandth	
1/2	a half	hemi semi demi
1/3	a third	
2/3	two thirds	
¼	a quarter	quadrant-
3/4	three quarters	
1/5	one fifth	
1/6	one sixth	sextant-
1/7	one seventh	
1/8	one eighth	
1/9	one ninth	

Whole Numbers

number	in words	prefix
0	zero	
1	one	uni-　　mono-
2	two	bi-　　di-
3	three	tri-
4	four	quad-　　tetra-
5	five	quin-　　pent-
6	six	hexa-
7	seven	sept-　　hepta-
8	eight	oct-
9	nine	nov-
10	ten	deca-
11	eleven	undec-
12	twelve	duodec-
13	thirteen	tredec-
14	fourteen	quattuordec-
15	fifteen	quindec-　quinquadec-
16	sixteen	sedec-
17	seventeen	septendec-
18	eighteen	octodec-
19	nineteen	novemdec-
20	twenty	viginti-
21	twenty-one	

number	in words	prefix
20	twenty	
30	thirty	triginti-
40	forty	quadraginti-
50	fifty	quinquaginti-
60	sixty	sexaginti-
70	seventy	septuaginti-
80	eighty	octoginti-
90	ninety	nonaginti-
100	one hundred	cent-
200	two hundred	ducenti-
300	three hundred	
400	four hundred	
500	five hundred	
600	six hundred	
700	seven hundred	
800	eight hundred	
900	nine hundred	
1000	one thousand	milli-
10000	ten thousand	
100000	one hundred thousand	
1000000	one million	mega-
1,000,000,000	one billion	
1,000,000,000,000	one trillion	

Prefixes which change a letter for assonance (to sound better)

prefix	prefix family	before base words which start with-	meaning
a- abs-	ab-	m c , t	away from, off
a- ac- ad- af- ag- al- an ap- ar- as- at-	ad-	sc, sp, st c , qu d f g l n p r s t	towards, near, in addition
ant-	anti-	vowels, h, consonant	against, opposed to
aut-	auto-	most vowels	self, same

co- col- com- cor- con-	com-	vowels, h, gn l m r, b, p, m remaining consonants	with, together

de-
di-
dif-
dis-
	dis-	all consonants
		b , d, l , m
		<n> <r> <s> <v>
		<g> <j>
		<f>
		<s>
			1. opposite,
			   not,
			   separate
			2. two
			3. exclude

el- em- en-	en-	l b , m , p	1. in 2. put in, on, onto
e- ec- ef- ex-	ex-	many consonants consonants f vowels, c, p , qu, s , t	out of, without, from
extra- extro-	extra-	vowels, consonant variant of above	outside, beyond, besides

il- im- in- ir-	in-	l b , m , p most consonants r	1.in, on, into, against 2.not
ob- oc- of- op-	ob-	most consonants c f p	toward, against, in the way
re- red-	re-	consonants vowels	1.back, in return 2.again
sub- suc- suf-- sug- sum- sup- sur- sus-	sub-	words from Latin c f g m p r s	under, below, beneath, secondary
syl- sym- syn- sys-	syn-	l b, m , p vowels, ch ,c d, t, th <s>	together, similarity

Suffixes

suffix	meaning	example
-acity (Fr.)	quality	veracity
-acy (L. and Gr.)	state, quality	fallacy
-ade (L.)	1. action, process 2. collective noun	1. blockade 2. decade
-age (M.E)	1. words from Fr. 2. words from verbs 3. amount of money	1. language 2. breakage 3. postage
-al (L.)	nouns of action from relevant verb	referral
-an	person	artisan
-ance (F. from L.)	action, state, quality	distance
-ancy (L.)	action, state, quality	buoyancy
-ant (Fr. from L.) and -ent	nouns of agency from relevant verb	servant
-ar (L.)	1. agent noun 2. from Latin words	1. beggar 2. collar
-arch (M.E)	chief	monarch
-archy (M.E)	rule, government	monarchy
-ard (M.E)	person (negative)	coward, drunkard
-arian (L.)	1. pursuits 2. age	1. antiquarian 2. septuagenarian
-art (M.E)	variant of -ard	braggart
-ary (L.)	1. location 2. function	1. dictionary 2. secretary
-ate (l.)	condition, office	senate
-ation (L.)	action, state, condition from verbs or adj. ending in -ate	separation
-chrome (Gr.)	colour	polychrome
-cracy	state	democracy
-crat (Gr.)	ruler	technocrat
-cule (Fr.)	diminutive	molecule
suffix	meaning	example

-cy (Fr.L.and Gr)	1.abstract nouns 2.rank	1.privacy 2.chaplaincy
-dom	1.collection of persons 2.domain 3.condition	1.officialdom 2. fiefdom 3. freedom
-ee	person who is the object of an action	refugee
-eer	person who works	profiteer
-en(O.E)	1.old plural ending 2.diminutive	1.brethren, children, oxen 2.kitten
-ence (F. from L.) = -ance	action, state, quality	difference
-ency -ancy	action, state, quality	agency
-ent variant of -ant	nouns of agency	dependent
-er (M.E)	1.agent nouns 2.people 3.action,process	1.teacher 2 butcher 3.dinner
-ery (M.E)	1. work, business 2.place 3.qualities	1. bakery 2.nunnery 3.prudery
-ess	female	waitress
-et (O.Fr)	diminutive	facet, islet
-ful (O.E.)	as much as will fill	spoonful
-gen (Fr.from Gr.)	1.s'th produced 2.s'th that produces	1.androgen 2.oxygen
-hood (M.E)	state, condition	statehood
-ia	1.collectives 2.diseases	1.militia 2.malaria
-iatry	healing	psychiatry
-ic (Gr.)	adjective nouns	public, magic
-ice (Fr from L)	state, quality	service
-ician	an expert	mathematician
-ics	body of facts	mathematics

-id (L.from Gr.)	belonging to a particular group	acid
-ie	1.endearment 2. Fr words	1. doggie 2. camaraderie, lingerie, menagerie, reverie
-ier (Fr.) and -eer	person who works	brigadier
-ility (Fr.from L)	abstract nouns	civility
-in (L.)	1.certain nouns 2. abstract nouns	1.cousin 2.ruin
-ine	meaning 'like a'	bovine
-ing	1.nouns from verb 2.nouns from other	1.building 2.shirting
-ion (L.) Also: -cion -sion, -ssion, -tion, -xion	state, condition, action, process things, people	suspicion tension, mission direction flexion
-isation	nouns from verbs ending in -ise	realisation
-is	1. Greek words 2. others	1.metropolis 2. tennis, trellis,
-ise	1.quality,function	1.merchandise
-ism	abstract noun of belief	communism
-ist	person	dentist
-ite 1.(Gr.)2.(L.)	1.tribe,doctrine 2.nouns from adj.	1.Laborite 2.opposite
-ition	nouns from verbs ending in -ite	expedition
-ity	abstract nouns of condition	civility
-ize	1.quality, function	prize
-let	diminutive	bracelet
-ling (O.E)	1. pejorative 2.diminutive	1.underling 2.duckling
-lith (Gr.)	stone	monolith
-ment (Fr.from L)	1.result of action 2.product	1.refreshment 2.fragment
-mony (L.)	result of action	parsimony
-ness (O.E)	state, quality	kindness

-ode (Gr.)	meaning 'the way'	electrode
-ol	nouns from chemicals	alcohol
-oma	tumour	carcinoma
-or	1.condition 2.person -work 3.alternative -our	1.error 2.doctor 3.candour
-ory (L.)	1. place 2. instrument	1.dormitory 2.dictionary
-osis (-oses Gr.)	action, process	metamorphosis
-osity	adj. of nouns in -ose	verbosity
-our variant of -o	condition, quality 1.from Fr. words -eur 2.from L. words -or	1.colour 2.labour
-path (Gr)	1.person who suffers from a disease 2.person who treats a disease	1. psychopath 2.naturopath
-pathy (Gr.)	1.suffering 2.disease	1.sympathy 2.neuropathy
-ply (M.E)	fold	three-ply
-ship (O.E)	status, condition	stewardship
-some (1.M.E 2.Gr)	1.with numerals 2. 'body'	1.twosome 2.chromosome
-speak (M.E)	jargon	adspeak
-ster (O.E)	persons (neg)	gangster
-teen (M.E)	numbers 13-19	thirteen
-th (O.E)	1.quality 2.related words 3.ordinal numbers	1. warmth 2.depth,length 3.fourth
-ton (Br.dialect)	person	simpleton
-tude (L.)	abstract nouns	attitude
-ty (M.E)	1.state, quality 2. numbers 20 +	1.unity 2. twenty
-ure (Fr.and L.)	abstract nouns	pressure
-y	1.diminutives 2.nouns from verbs	1.doggy 2.inquiry

suffix	nationalities
-an	Afghan, American, German, Mexican, Moroccan, South African, Tongan, Tibetan, Uruguayan
-ean	Chilean, Korean, New Guinean, Singaporean
-ian	Algerian, Australian, Austrian, Belgian, Bosnian, Brazilian, Cambodian, Canadian, Columbian, Egyptian, Estonian, Fijian, Hungarian, Indian, Indonesian, Iranian, Italian, Latvian, Lithuanian, Malaysian, New Caledonian, Norwegian
-ese	Burmese, Chinese, Congolese, Japanese, Nepalese, Portuguese, Sudanese, Taiwanese, Timorese
-ish	English, Finnish, Irish, Polish, Scottish, Spanish, Swedish, Turkish
-i	Bengali, Iraqi, Israeli, Omani, Pakistani, Saudi
-o	Filipino
-er	New Zealander
-ch	French
-sh	Welsh, Yiddish
-iss	Swiss
-ine	Argentine
-utch	Dutch
-ech	Czech
-ai	Thai
-iot	Cypriot
-k	Greek
-ic	Arabic, Amharic
-ew	Hebrew
-ao	Lao
suffix	nationalities

Verb Suffixes

suffix	meaning	example
-ate (L.)	from L. past participles	ruminate
-ed	regular past participle	looked
-en (M.E)	1.verbs from adj 2.past participles	1.fasten 2.taken
-er (M.E)	verbs of motion	flutter
-fy (Fr.from L.)	1.to cause to be 2.to be made	1.beautify 2.solidify
-efy variant	only occurs in four words	liquefy, putrefy, rarefy, stupefy
-ify	used when preceded by a consonant	modify
-ing	present participle	lying
-ise	1.type of action-can also use –ize 2.some verbs only in -ise	1.energise 2. compromise
-ize	1.type of action-can also use –ize 2.words from Greek 3 verbs only in -ize	1.energize 2.baptize 3.capsize,prize,seize
-le	verbs of repeated action	twinkle
-our	verb form of nouns in -our	(to) labour
-t	1. past tense or participle of certain verbs 2.alternative to -ed for some verbs	1.built 2. burnt, dreamt, learnt, spelt, spilt, spoilt
-ure	activity	manufacture

suffix	meaning	example
-able	ability	manageable
-ac	relating to something	cardiac
-al -ial -ical	connected with	annual judicial magical
-an -ian	belonging to a group	human Australian
-ane	variant of an adjective ending in -an	humane
-ant	common ending	pleasant
-ar -iar -ary	having to do with	columnar linear honorary
-ate	past participle adjectival ending	separate
-ed	adj. formed from the action of a verb	inflated
-en	material, appearance	wooden , golden
-er	comparative adjective	bigger
-ern	adjectival suffix	northern, southern
-esque	style, manner	picturesque
-est	superlative adjective	biggest
-facient	causes	absorbefacient
-fic	making	horrific
-fid	divided	bicuspid
-ful	1. full of 2. tending to	1. wonderful 2. wakeful
-genous	from nouns ending in -gen	homogenous
-ible	variant of -able, especially in words from Latin	legible

suffix	meaning	example
-ic	having to do with	metallic
-ical	forms adjectives from nouns ending in -ic	rhetorical
-id	to do with the senses	acrid , acid
-il	-ile capability civil	agile
-in	indicates a pharmaceutical substance	asprin
-ing	present participle	thinking
-ish	1.nationalities 2.'like' 3.'rather'	1.English 2.girlish 3. sweetish
-istic	from nouns ending in -ist	nationalistic
-ite	adjective from verbs	composite
-ive -ative -itive	tending to be	active talkative punitive
-less	'without'	colourless
-like	'like'	childlike
suffix	meaning	example

suffix	meaning	example
-ly	'like'	manly
-ory	'the function of'	illusory
-ose	'full of'	verbose
-otic	from nouns ending in -osis	hypnotic
-ous -eous -ious	'full of' having the nature of	nervous gaseous fractious
-some	tendency to	troublesome
-ulent	having a lot of	fraudulent
-ulous	tendency to	populous
worthy	'worthy of'	trustworthy
-y	characterised by	chilly

Adverbial Suffixes

suffixes	meaning	example
-fold	multiply or increase	manifold
-ly	1. usual way to form adverbs from adj. 2. added to units of time	1. happily 2. hourly
-ward	direction	homeward
-ways	direction	lengthways
-wise	1. attitude 2. direction 3. 'with respect to'	1. likewise 2. lengthwise 3. moneywise

Common medical and nursing phrases

Noun	Verb	Adjective
abnormality		abnormal
absence of fever	be afebrile	afebrile
absence of fever	be apyrexical	apyrexical
administration	administer	administrative
allergy	suffer from allergies be allergic to	allergic
ambulation	ambulate	ambulant / ambulatory
anaemia	suffer from anaemia	anaemic
anorexia	be anorexic	anorexic
anticoagulation		anticoagulant
anxiety	suffer from anxiety	anxious
artery		arterial
asepsis		aseptic
assessment	assess	assessed
aspiration	aspirate	aspirated
asthma	suffer from asthma	asthmatic
auscultation	auscultate	
blindness sight impairment	be blind suffer from sight impairment	blind sight impaired
bradycardia	be bradycardic	bradycardic
breathing	breathe	
cannulation	cannulate	cannulated
cartilage		cartilaginous

Noun	Verb	Adjective
catheter	catheterise	catheterised
caution	be cautious	cautious
Coeliac Disease	suffer from Coeliac disease	coeliac
coma	be in a coma / be comatose	comatose
communication	communicate	communicative
confusion	confuse	confused
consciousness	be conscious	conscious
constipation	constipate	constipated
continence	be continent	continent of urine / faeces
contraception	use contraception	contraceptive
co-operation	co-operate	co-operative
co-ordination	co-ordinate	co-ordinated
deafness hearing impairment	suffer from deafness suffer from a hearing impairment	deaf hearing impaired
degeneration	degenerate	degenerative
dementia	suffer from dementia	demented
depression	feel depressed	depressive
developmental delay	be developmentally delayed	developmentally delayed
diabetes	suffer from diabetes	diabetic
diagnosis	diagnose	diagnostic
diarrhoea	suffer from diarrhoea	none
diet	diet	dietary
digestion	digest	digestive
distension	distend	distended
dizziness		dizzy

Noun	Verb	Adjective
drowsiness	feel drowsy	drowsy
elimination	eliminate	eliminated
emaciation	emaciate	emaciated
emotion		emotional
euthanasia	euthanize	euthanized
exacerbation	exacerbate	exacerbated
expiration	expire	expiratory
exposure	exposed to	exposed
extension	extend	extended
faeces	pass faeces	faecal
failure	fail	failing
flexion	flex	flexed
haemophilia	suffer from haemophilia	haemophiliac
hydration	hydrate	hydrating
hyperglycaemic attacks	suffer from hyperglycaemic attacks	hyperglycaemic
hypoglycaemic attacks	suffer from hypoglycaemic attacks	hypoglycaemic
illness	fall ill / be ill	ill
immobility	be immobile	immobile
incontinent	be incontinent	incontinent of urine / faeces
induction	induce	induced
infection	have an infection be infectious	infectious infective
inflammation	be inflamed	inflamed
inhibition	inhibit	inhibiting

Noun	Verb	Adjective
insomnia	suffer from insomnia	insomniac
inspiration	inspire	inspiratory
instability	be unstable	unstable
intensity	be intensive	intensive
intervention	intervene	intervening
intoxication	intoxicate	intoxicated
interaction	interact with	interactive
intubation	intubate	intubated
itchiness	be itchy	itchy
mania		manic
manipulation	manipulate	manipulative (person)
metabolism	metabolise	metabolised
mobilisation	mobilise	mobilising
mobility	be mobile	mobile
monitoring	monitor	monitored
muscle		muscular
nausea	experience nausea feel sick	nauseated sick
normality		normal
nourishment	nourish	nourishing
nutrition		nutritious
obesity	be obese	obese
overweight	be overweight	overweight
oxygenation	oxygenate	oxygenating
pain	experience pain be in pain	painful

Noun	Verb	Adjective
absence of pain	be pain-free	pain-free
palliation	palliate	palliative
phobia	suffer from (type) phobia	(type) phobic
photosensitivity	suffers from photosensitivity	photosensitive
precautions	take precautions	
progression	progress	progressive
prophylaxis		prophylactic
provision	provide	provided
psychology		psychological
psychosis		psychotic
pyrexia	be pyrexical	pyrexical
dyspnoea / shortness of breath	suffer from dyspnoea/ shortness of breath	dyspnoeic/ short of breath
relapse	relapse	relapsing
remission	be in remission	
respiration	respire	respiratory
response responsiveness	respond to	responsive
restriction	restrict	restrictive
retention	retain	retentive
secretions	secrete	secreting
sedation	sedate	sedative
soreness	be sore	sore
spasm	have spasms	spasmodic
stability	provide stability	stable
sterility	be sterile	sterile

Noun	Verb	Adjective
stress	to be stressed	stressful
stroke	have suffered a stroke	stroke- affected
support	support	supportive
suppression	suppress	suppressed
sweating	sweat	sweating
tachycardia	be tachycardic	tachycardic
tension	be tense	tense
termination (of pregnancy)	terminate (a pregnancy) have a termination	terminated (pregnancy) terminal (illness)
transfer	transfer	transferring
trauma	suffer trauma	traumatic
treatment	treat with	treated
underweight		underweight
urine	pass urine	urinary
vasoconstriction	vasoconstrict	vasoconstricting
vasodilation	vasodilate	vasodilating
vein		venous
weakness	weaken	weak
withdrawal	withdraw from	withdrawn

Glossary of Hospital Terms

- Receptacles
- Vital Signs
- Glasgow Coma Scale
- Fluid Balance Chart
- Bristol Stool Chart
- Waterlow Pressure Area Assessment
- Assessment of ADLs
- Falls Risk Assessment
- MUST
- Oral Assessment
- Pain Assessment
- PCA
- Oxygen
- VIPS
- Wound Care
- Incident Report
- Medication
- Manual Handling
- Dental

Washing	
wash bowl	used to give a bed bath
wash basin	attached to the wall, to wash hands
linen cupboard	area where clean linen is kept, fire-safe if necessary
linen skip	receptacle for soiled linen, usually on wheels
cotton blanket	easily washable blanket
hand gel	alcohol-based hand wash
cleansing foam	alcohol-based hand wash liquid

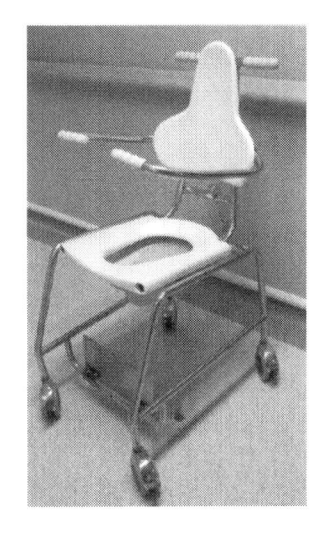

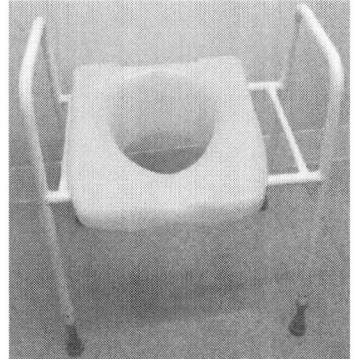

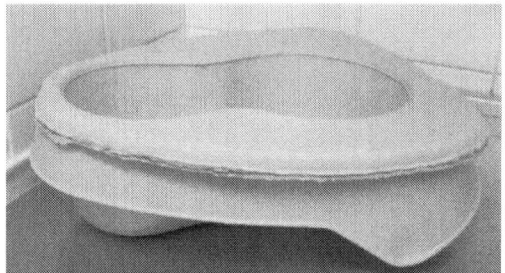

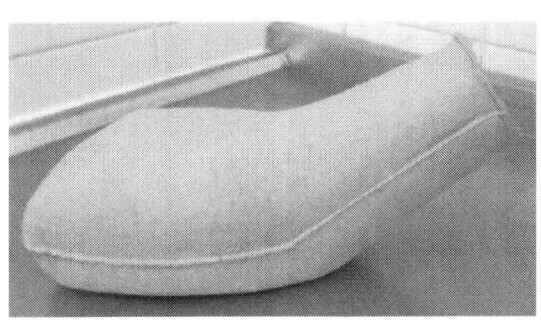

Toileting	
commode chair	toilet seat on wheels which can have a bedpan placed under it or be wheeled over a toilet
raised toilet seat	toilet seat which has been raised to make it easier for patients to sit on the toilet after hip surgery
incontinence sheet	thin absorbent sheet placed under areas where leakage may occur e.g leakage of any body fluids
(incontinence) pad	thick pad to collect urine or faeces of incontinent patients
(urinary) catheter	tube inserted into the bladder to drain urine into a bag
catheter bag	closed sterile bag which receives urine via a catheter tube
urinal	also called 'bottle', receptacle for men to pass urine into
bed pan	receptacle which is placed under the buttocks of bed-bound patients so they can go to the toilet
slipper pan	a thin bed pan

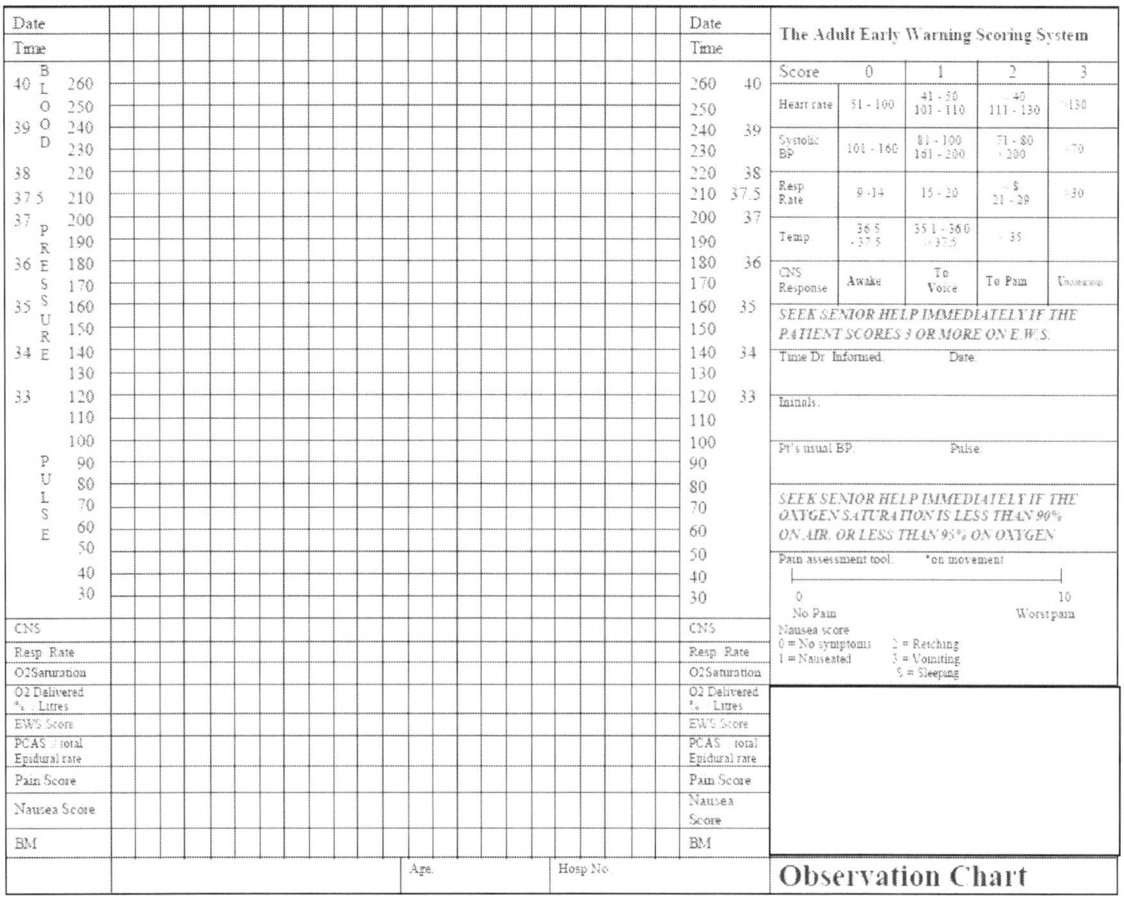

Date																Date		The Adult Early Warning Scoring System
Time																Time		

Score	0	1	2	3
Heart rate	51 - 100	41 - 50 / 101 - 110	40 / 111 - 130	>130
Systolic BP	101 - 160	81 - 100 / 161 - 200	71 - 80 / >200	<70
Resp Rate	9 - 14	15 - 20	<8 / 21 - 29	>30
Temp	36.5 - 37.5	35.1 - 36.0 / >37.5	<35	
CNS Response	Awake	To Voice	To Pain	Unconscious

SEEK SENIOR HELP IMMEDIATELY IF THE PATIENT SCORES 3 OR MORE ON E.W.S.

Time Dr Informed: Date:

Initials:

Pt's usual BP: Pulse:

SEEK SENIOR HELP IMMEDIATELY IF THE OXYGEN SATURATION IS LESS THAN 90% ON AIR, OR LESS THAN 95% ON OXYGEN

Pain assessment tool: *on movement*

0 ————————————————— 10
No Pain   Worst pain

Nausea score
0 = No symptoms   2 = Retching
1 = Nauseated   3 = Vomiting
                             S = Sleeping

Observation Chart

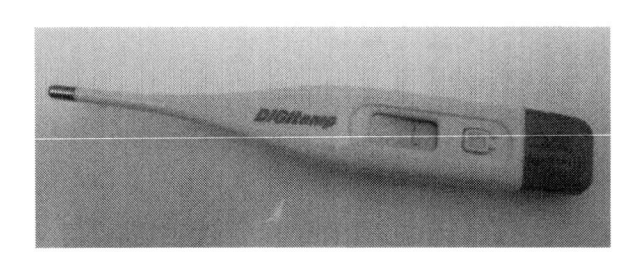

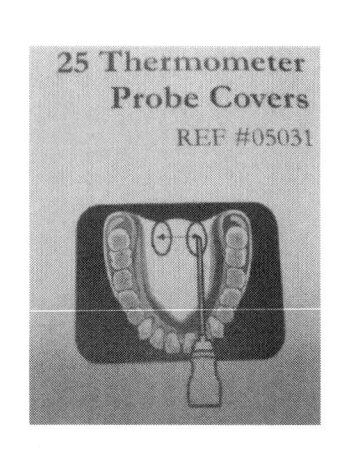

25 Thermometer Probe Covers
REF #05031

Vital Signs

temperature	measurement of body heat
thermometer	device used to measure a patient's temperature
thermometer probe cover	clean covering placed over a metal probe before placing it in a patient's mouth
axillary per axilla	under the armpit
oral	by mouth
sublingual	under the tongue
rectally or per rectum	into the rectum or back passage
tympanic	in the ear
afebrile or apyrexical	without a fever
febrile pyrexia pyrexical	having a fever
rigors	shivering which occurs with fevers
hypothermic	abnormally low temperature
hyperthermic	abnormally high temperature
pulse	heart rate
bradycardia	slow pulse
tachycardia	fast pulse
thready	type of weak pulse
bounding	type of fast pulse
irregular	not regular e.g. missing a beat

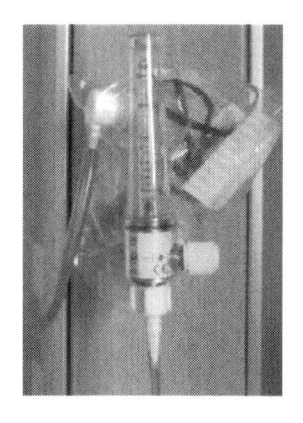

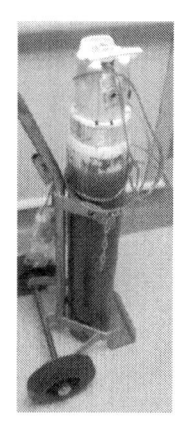

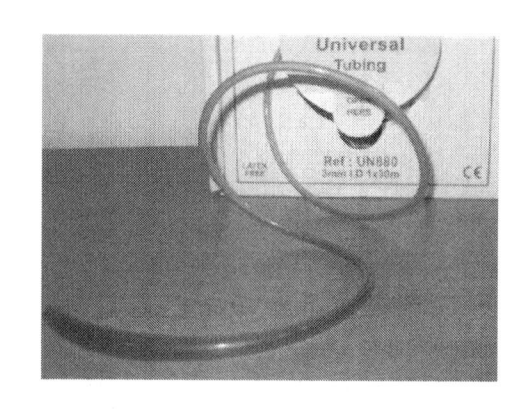

term	meaning
temporal pulse	pulse at the temples
carotid pulse	pulse on either side of the neck
apex pulse	pulse at the apex of the heart
brachial pulse	pulse at the antecubital fossa in the elbow
posterior tibial pulse)	pulse next to the ankle - checked in a patient with peripheral vascular disease
dorsalis pedis pulse	pulse on top of the foot ,next to the navicular bone
radial pulse	pulse at the wrist
popliteal pulse	pulse behind the knee
femoral pulse	pulse in the groin
respirations or resps respiratory rate	breaths ,breathing the rate or speed of breathing
apnoea (apnea)	without / no breathing ,absence of breathing
tachypnoea (tachypnea)	fast breathing rate i.e a rate over 24
bradypnoea (bradypnea)	slow breathing rate (under 16 breaths per minute) or depressed respiratory rate
Cheyne Stokes breathing Cheyne Stoking	slow, irregular breathing at the end of life
Kussmaul breathing	laboured breathing seen in diabetic acidosis

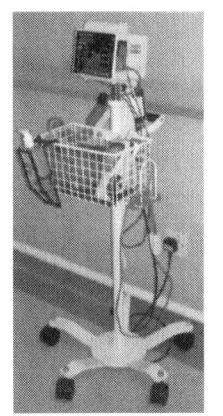

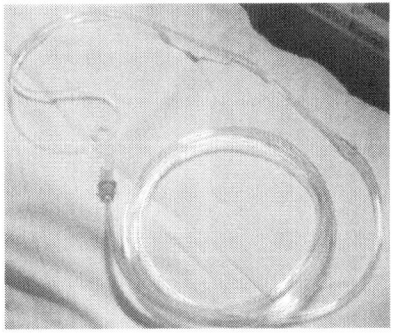

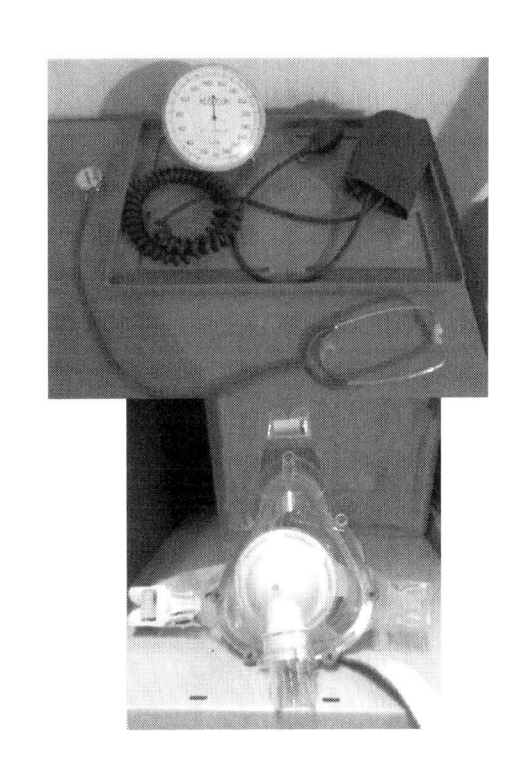

term	meaning
digital monitor	digital device which measures Vital Signs (BP,P , oxygen sats and temperature
sphygmomanometer	a manual device used to take blood pressure
pulse oximetry pulse oximeter	method of assessing level of oxygenation in the blood device used to give oxygen sats readings
oxygen cylinder	a receptacle where oxygen is stored under pressure
nasal cannulae	nasal prongs, nasal specs (short for spectacles)
oxygen mask	cover for nose and mouth to allow delivery of oxygen from an oxygen supply to the patient
nebuliser mask	mask which allows a fine mist of asthma medication to be delivered to the patient
CPAP Continuous Positive Air Pressure	A device which delivers a small amount of air into the nose to keep the airway open while a person sleeps
blood pressure	pressure of blood on blood vessel walls
hypertension	systolic over 140 and diastolic over 90 for 3 consecutive readings
hypotension	systolic less than 100

Glasgow Coma Scale - excerpt

PAIN ASSESSMENT
Please ask, When you raise your head or cough gently, do you experience

0 = No Pain
1 = Mild
2 = Moderate
3 = Severe

NAUSEA SCORE

0 = No Nausea
N = Nausea
V = Vomiting

110
100
90
80
70
60
50

RESPS
SA O$_2$
%O$_2$ Given

Pupil Scale (mm)
- 10mm
- 9mm
- 8mm
- 7mm
- 6mm
- 5mm
- 4mm
- 3mm
- 2mm
- 1mm

COMA SCALE

EYES OPEN	4	SPONTANEOUSLY	
	3	TO SPEECH	
	2	TO PAIN	
	1	NONE	
BEST VERBAL RESPONSE	5	ORIENTATED	
	4	CONFUSED	
	3	INAPPROPRIATE WORDS	
	2	INCOMPREHENSIBLE SOUNDS	
	1	NONE	
BEST MOTOR RESPONSE	6	OBEY COMMANDS	
	5	LOCALISE TO PAIN	
	4	WITHDRAWS TO PAIN	
	3	FLEXION TO PAIN	
	2	EXTENSION TO PAIN	
	1	NONE	

LIMB MOVEMENTS

ARMS:
- NORMAL POWER
- MILD WEAKNESS
- SEVERE WEAKNESS
- FLEXION
- EXTENSION
- NONE

LEGS:
- NORMAL POWER
- MILD WEAKNESS
- SEVERE WEAKNESS
- FLEXION
- EXTENSION
- NONE

PUPILS
- ✓ Reacts
- ✓ Sluggish
- — None

R C = CLOSED   SIZE   REACTION
L C = CLOSED   SIZE   REACTION

PAEDIATRIC PATIENTS

BEST MOTOR RESPONSE
- SPONTANEOUS OR OBEYS VERBAL COMMAND 6
- LOCALISES PAIN 5
- WITHDRAWS IN RESPONSE TO PAIN 4
- ABNORMAL FLEXION TO PAIN 3
- ABNORMAL EXTENSION TO PAIN 2
- NO RESPONSE 1

BEST VERBAL RESPONSE
Smiles, orientatedto sounds interacts, follows objects 5

CRYING:
- CONSOLABLE
- INCONSISTENTLY CONSOLABLE
- INCONSOLABLE
- NO RESPONSE

INTERACTS:
- INAPPROPRIATE 4
- MOANING 3
- IRRITABLE 2
- NO RESPONSE 1

GLASGOW COMA SCALE

Glasgow Coma Scale	
neurology neurological	study of the nervous system
observation observe	to watch for specific information
pupil	black central area of the eyeball
spontaneous	something which happens on its own
orientation orientated	The patient knows where s/he is and what the date and time is.
inappropriate appropriate	The patient says things which do not relate to the topic things relate to the topic
incomprehensible comprehensible	does not make sense makes sense
obeys commands disobeys commands	follows an instruction The patient does not do what is asked of them
power	strength of a limb (arm or leg)
weakness to be weak strength to be strong (opp)	not have any power e.g muscle weakness have power
flexion to flex	bend a limb
extension to extend	straighten out a limb
pupil reaction	the ways pupils react after a light is shone onto them
brisk reaction	quick reaction
sluggish reaction	slow reaction

Fluid Balance Chart

DAILY INTAKE-OUTPUT CHART
(Not to be filed in Medical Record)

Surname Mr./Mrs./Miss: _____
First Names: _____
Case No.: _____

Bodyweight ....

24hrs. from .... on .... to .... on ....

INSTRUCTIONS FOR 24 HOURS (PARENTERAL)
All intravenous fluid therapy and drug additives to these fluids must be prescribed on the "INTRAVENOUS FLUIDS AND DRUG ADDITIVES" form provided. Please refer to this form for fluid volumes which will be required when completing the INTAKE section below. (H.M.R. 111(W) IV).
NOTE The "Type" heading below refers to the particular fluid prescribed in the numbered section on the "INTRAVENOUS FLUID AND DRUG ADDITIVES" form.

INSTRUCTIONS FOR 24 HOURS (ORAL)

TIME	INTAKE						OUTPUT				
	INTRAVENOUS FLUIDS			ORAL		Other	URINE		Gastric		Drainage	Other
	Type	Vol. set up	given vol.	Vol.	Type	Vol.	Vol.	S.G.	Vol.	Nature	Vol.	Vol.
c/f												
12 hour Total												
12 hour Total												
12 hour Total												

CUMULATIVE BALANCE   +   −

H.M.R 210A (W)82 (WKJ120X)

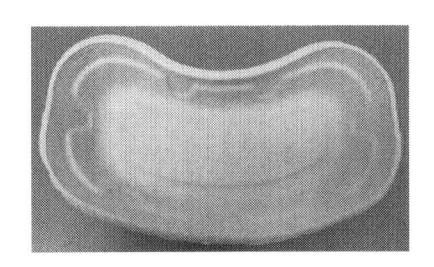

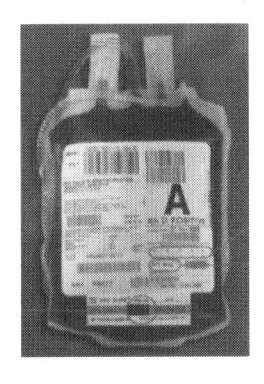

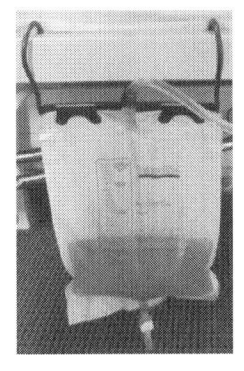

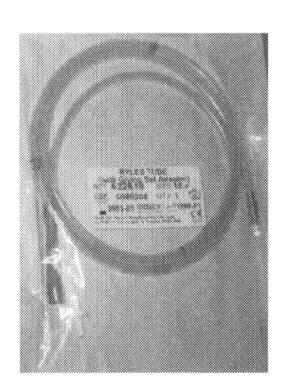

Fluid Balance Chart	
homeostasis	equal fluid balance ,equal intake and output
oral intake	any fluids which are taken by mouth
parenteral	delivered as an injection
IV fluids	any fluids which are administered through an intravenous cannula
blood transfusion	a bag filled with blood which is administered through an intravenous cannula
vomitus to vomit emesis	fluid which is discharged from the body as vomitus or emesis
vomit bowl	also a kidney dish: receptacle to hold vomitus
urine to pass urine	waste fluid passed out of the body through the urethra
naso-gastric tube Ryles tube	tube placed into the stomach via the nose
aspirate	fluid which is syringed out of a naso-gastric tube
faecal output	liquid passed from the body as diarrhoea through the rectum or through a stoma.

Bristol Stool Chart

Type 1	Separate hard lumps, like nuts (hard to pass)
Type 2	Sausage-shaped but lumpy
Type 3	Like a sausage but with cracks on its surface
Type 4	Like a sausage or snake, smooth and soft
Type 5	Soft blobs with clear-cut edges (passed easily)
Type 6	Fluffy pieces with ragged edges, a mushy stool
Type 7	Watery, no solid pieces, **Entirely Liquid**

bowel movement / have one's bowels open	go to the toilet to empty the contents of the bowel
faeces faecal matter	waste products of the body which are usually passed through the rectum
stool , pass a stool	faecal matter from one bowel movement
stool specimen	small amount of faeces which is sent to a laboratory for testing
constipation be constipated	not able to open your bowels
faecal impaction be impacted	Also called faecal loading , the bowel obstructed with faeces which cannot be passed
diarrhoea have diarrhoea	loose bowel motions
colostomy	surgical opening on the outside of the abdomen which allows excretion of faeces
stoma	surgical opening made to allow drainage of body fluids if normal routes cannot be used
fluff fluffy	faeces which is light and frothy
lump lumpy	faeces which is irregularly-shaped
mush mushy	faeces which is soft and pulpy in consistency
water watery	liquid faeces which is colourless or near colourless

WATERLOW PRESSURE ULCER RISK ASSESSMENT TOOL

Add totals to obtain risk score. Several scores per category can be calculated.

Has the patient previously had a pressure ulcer? **Yes**   **No**

SEX/AGE		BUILD/WEIGHT FOR HEIGHT		SPECIAL RISKS	
Male	1	**BMI**		**TISSUE MALNUTRITION**	
Female	2	Average (20 – 24.9)	0	Terminal cachexia	8
14-49	1	Above average (25 – 29.9)	1	Multiple organ failure	8
50-64	2	Obese > 30	2	Single organ failure ie.	5
65-74	3	Below average < 20	3	(resp. renal, cardiac & liver)	
75-80	4			Peripheral vascular disease	5
81+	5	BMI = WT (Kg) / HT (m²)		Anaemia (Hb<8)	2
				Smoking	1
MOBILITY		**CONTINENCE**		**NEUROLOGICAL DEFICIT**	
Fully	0	Complete/catheterised	0	Diabetes, MS, CVA,	4 - 6
Restless/fidgety	1	Urine incontinence	1	Motor/sensory paraplegia	
Apathetic	2	Faecal incontinence	2	(maximum of 6)	
Restricted	3	Urinary and faecal incontinence	3	**MAJOR SURGERY OR TRAUMA**	
Bedbound (eg. traction)	4			Orthopaedic/Spinal	5
				On table > 2hrs (past 48hrs)	5
Chairbound (eg. wheelchair)	5			> 6hrs (past 48hrs)	8
NUTRITIONAL STATUS		**SKIN TYPE VISUAL RISK AREAS**		**MEDICATION**	
Nutritional score from Malnutrition screening tool below		Healthy	0	Cytotoxics	
		Tissue paper	1	Steroids	4
		Dry	1	Anti-inflammatory	
		Oedematous	1		
		Clammy, pyrexia	1	(maximum of 4)	
		Discoloured Stage 1	2		
		Pressure ulcer Stage 2-4	3		

Abbreviations	Meaning
BMI	Body Mass Index
WT	weight
HT	height
kg	kilogram
m²	square metres
Hb	haemoglobin
resp.	respiratory
MS	multiple sclerosis
CVA	cerebrovascular accident. Also called CVE cerebrovascular event

BRADEN SCALE FOR PREDICTING PRESSURE SORE RISK

Patient's Name _____ Evaluator's Name _____ Date of Assessment _____

SENSORY PERCEPTION ability to respond meaningfully to pressure-related discomfort	1. Completely Limited Unresponsive (does not moan, flinch, or grasp) to painful stimuli, due to diminished level of consciousness or sedation. OR limited ability to feel pain over most of body	2. Very Limited Responds only to painful stimuli. Cannot communicate discomfort except by moaning or restlessness OR has a sensory impairment which limits the ability to feel pain or discomfort over ½ of body.	3. Slightly Limited Responds to verbal commands, but cannot always communicate discomfort or the need to be turned. OR has some sensory impairment which limits ability to feel pain or discomfort in 1 or 2 extremities.	4. No Impairment Responds to verbal commands. Has no sensory deficit which would limit ability to feel or voice pain or discomfort.
MOISTURE degree to which skin is exposed to moisture	1. Constantly Moist Skin is kept moist almost constantly by perspiration, urine, etc. Dampness is detected every time patient is moved or turned.	2. Very Moist Skin is often, but not always moist. Linen must be changed at least once a shift.	3. Occasionally Moist: Skin is occasionally moist, requiring an extra linen change approximately once a day.	4. Rarely Moist Skin is usually dry, linen only requires changing at routine intervals.
ACTIVITY degree of physical activity	1. Bedfast Confined to bed.	2. Chairfast Ability to walk severely limited or non-existent. Cannot bear own weight and/or must be assisted into chair or wheelchair.	3. Walks Occasionally Walks occasionally during day, but for very short distances, with or without assistance. Spends majority of each shift in bed or chair	4. Walks Frequently Walks outside room at least twice a day and inside room at least once every two hours during waking hours
MOBILITY ability to change and control body position	1. Completely Immobile Does not make even slight changes in body or extremity position without assistance	2. Very Limited Makes occasional slight changes in body or extremity position but unable to make frequent or significant changes independently.	3. Slightly Limited Makes frequent though slight changes in body or extremity position independently.	4. No Limitation Makes major and frequent changes in position without assistance.
NUTRITION usual food intake pattern	1. Very Poor Never eats a complete meal. Rarely eats more than ⅓ of any food offered. Eats 2 servings or less of protein (meat or dairy products) per day. Takes fluids poorly. Does not take a liquid dietary supplement OR is NPO and/or maintained on clear liquids or IV's for more than 5 days.	2. Probably Inadequate Rarely eats a complete meal and generally eats only about ½ of any food offered. Protein intake includes only 3 servings of meat or dairy products per day. Occasionally will take a dietary supplement. OR receives less than optimum amount of liquid diet or tube feeding	3. Adequate Eats over half of most meals. Eats a total of 4 servings of protein (meat, dairy products) per day. Occasionally will refuse a meal, but will usually take a supplement when offered OR is on a tube feeding or TPN regimen which probably meets most of nutritional needs.	4. Excellent Eats most of every meal. Never refuses a meal. Usually eats a total of 4 or more servings of meat and dairy products. Occasionally eats between meals. Does not require supplementation.
FRICTION & SHEAR	1. Problem Requires moderate to maximum assistance in moving. Complete lifting without sliding against sheets is impossible. Frequently slides down in bed or chair, requiring frequent repositioning with maximum assistance. Spasticity, contractures or agitation leads to almost constant friction	2. Potential Problem Moves feebly or requires minimum assistance. During a move skin probably slides to some extent against sheets, chair, restraints or other devices. Maintains relatively good position in chair or bed most of the time but occasionally slides down.	3. No Apparent Problem Moves in bed and in chair independently and has sufficient muscle strength to lift up completely during move. Maintains good position in bed or chair.	

noun	verb	adjective
anaemia	be anaemic	anaemic
apathy	be apathetic	apathetic
	be bed-bound be bed-fast	bed bound bed fast
blood vessel		vascular
cachexia	be cachectic	cachectic
catheterisation	catheterise	catheterised
	be chair-bound be chair-fast	chair bound chair fast
comfort discomfort	be comfortable with be uncomfortable with	comfortable uncomfortable
continence incontinence	be continent be incontinent	continent incontinent
dampness	dampen with be damp	damp

deficit	be deficient in	deficient in
discolouration	discolour something be discoloured	discoloured
faeces	pass faeces	faecal
failure	fail	failing
fidgetiness	fidget around	fidgety
friction	cause friction	
impairment	impair	impaired
nutrition malnutrition	nourish be well / poorly nourished	well nourished malnourished
moisture	moisten be moist	moist
motion	move	motor
oedema (edema)	be oedematous	oedematous
paraplegia	be paraplegic	paraplegic
(on the) periphery		peripheral
perspiration	perspire	
pressure area	press down on	pressured
response lack of response	respond to not respond to	responsive unresponsive
restlessness	be restless	restless
restriction	restrict be restricted	restricted
sedation	sedate someone with	sedated
the senses	sense	sensory
shearing	shear	shearing
termination	terminate	terminal
urine	pass urine	urinary

ADLS Activities of Daily Living

Completed following discussion with the Care Team						
Activities of Daily Living Observations (Care Staff)						
Key: IND = Independent SA = Some assistance FA = Full assistance GD = Guide & direct SUP = Supervision N/A = Not applicable						
Vision & Hearing Aids						
Fitting/removing hearing aid(s)	IND	SA	FA	G&D	SUP	N/A
Cleaning hearing aid(s)	IND	SA	FA	G&D	SUP	N/A
Changing hearing aid batteries	IND	SA	FA	G&D	SUP	N/A
Fitting/removing glasses	IND	SA	FA	G&D	SUP	N/A
Cleaning glasses	IND	SA	FA	G&D	SUP	N/A
Overall aids assessment	IND	SA	FA	G&D	SUP	N/A
Moving in Bed						
Turn in bed	IND	SA	FA	G&D	SUP	N/A
Sit up in bed	IND	SA	FA	G&D	SUP	N/A
Get out of bed	IND	SA	FA	G&D	SUP	N/A
Eat/Drink while in bed	IND	SA	FA	G&D	SUP	N/A
Locate/use call bell in bed	IND	SA	FA	G&D	SUP	N/A
Overall bed mobility assessment	IND	SA	FA	G&D	SUP	N/A
Using the Toilet						
Find the toilet/commode	IND	SA	FA	G&D	SUP	N/A
Adjust clothes	IND	SA	FA	G&D	SUP	N/A
Position self on toilet safely	IND	SA	FA	G&D	SUP	N/A
Wipe peri area after toilet	IND	SA	FA	G&D	SUP	N/A
Flush the toilet	IND	SA	FA	G&D	SUP	N/A
Wash hands after toilet	IND	SA	FA	G&D	SUP	N/A
Change/place incontinence pad	IND	SA	FA	G&D	SUP	N/A
Overall toileting assessment	IND	SA	FA	G&D	SUP	N/A
Eating & Drinking						
Apply clothing protector	IND	SA	FA	G&D	SUP	N/A
Use knife, fork & spoon	IND	SA	FA	G&D	SUP	N/A
Drink from cup	IND	SA	FA	G&D	SUP	N/A
Commence, continue, complete meal	IND	SA	FA	G&D	SUP	N/A
Overall eating and drinking assessment	IND	SA	FA	G&D	SUP	N/A

fit hearing aid	place hearing aid into outer ear and switch on
fit glasses	put on glasses
locate call bell	find call bell
adjust clothes	tuck in shirt and ensure clothes are comfortable
position self on the toilet	sit on the toilet seat safely
wipe peri area	clean the perineal area
flush the toilet	push button or handle to enable water to clean toilet bowl
apply clothing protector	put on a bib or long napkin

ACTIVITIES POINTS (1 OR 0)	INDEPENDENCE: (1 POINT) NO supervision, direction or personal assistance	DEPENDENCE: (0 POINTS) WITH supervision, direction, personal assistance or total care
BATHING POINTS:_____	(1 POINT) Bathes self completely or needs help in bathing only a single part of the body such as the back, genital area or disabled extremity.	(0 POINTS) Needs help with bathing more than one part of the body, getting in or out of the tub or shower. Requires total bathing.
DRESSING POINTS:_____	(1 POINT) Gets clothes from closets and drawers and puts on clothes and outer garments complete with fasteners. May have help tying shoes.	(0 POINTS) Needs help with dressing self or needs to be completely dressed.
TOILETING POINTS:_____	(1 POINT) Goes to toilet, gets on and off, arranges clothes, cleans genital area without help.	(0 POINTS) Needs help transferring to the toilet, cleaning self or uses bedpan or commode.
TRANSFERRING POINTS:_____	(1 POINT) Moves in and out of bed or chair unassisted. Mechanical transferring aides are acceptable.	(0 POINTS) Needs help in moving from bed to chair or requires a complete transfer.
CONTINENCE POINTS:_____	(1 POINT) Exercises complete self control over urination and defecation.	(0 POINTS) Is partially or totally incontinent of bowel or bladder.
FEEDING POINTS:_____	(1 POINT) Gets food from plate into mouth without help. Preparation of food may be done by another person.	(0 POINTS) Needs partial or total help with feeding or requires parenteral feeding.

TOTAL POINTS = _____ 6 = High (*patient independent*) 0 = Low (*patient very dependent*)

ADLs	Activities of Daily Living
independent with ADLs	able to perform ADLs without assistance
supervise with ADLs	minor assistance needed with ADLs
dependent	needs help
independent	does not need help
transferring	moving from one place to another e.g. from bed to chair
continence	ability to pass urine and faeces into a toilet or commode
incontinence	leakage of body fluids onto clothing or bedding
feeding	ability to take in food and drink

Falls Risk

FALL RISK STATUS: *(Circle)*: LOW / MEDIUM / HIGH	List Fall Status on Care Plan/ Flow Chart
IMPORTANT: IF **HIGH**, *COMMENCE FALL ALERT*	

PART 2: RISK FACTOR CHECKLIST

		Y/N
Vision	Reports / observed difficulty seeing - objects / signs / finding way around	
Mobility	Mobility status unknown or appears unsafe / impulsive / forgets gait aid	
Transfers	Transfer status unknown or appears unsafe ie. over-reaches, impulsive	
Behaviours	Observed or reported agitation, confusion, disorientation	
	Difficulty following instructions or non-compliant (observed or known)	
Activities of Daily Living (A.D.L's)	Observed risk-taking behaviours, or reported from referrer / previous facility	
	Observed unsafe use of equipment	
	Unsafe footwear / inappropriate clothing	
Environment	Difficulties with orientation to environment i.e. areas between bed / bathroom / dining room	
Nutrition	Underweight / low appetite	
Continence	Reported or known urgency / nocturia / accidents	
Other		

falls	any accidental falling over e.g because unsteady on feet
fall alert	means of telling staff to be careful regarding the likelihood of the patient falling
trips	accidental falling over an object in the way of a person
slips	accidental sliding and falling usually related to liquid on the floor
risk (of)	the probability that something may happen
at risk (patient)	a patient who is at risk of something e.g falls
status	classification of the severity of risk e.g low risk status
impulsive	actions taken before careful consideration
gait aid	also called walking aid e.g walking stick
over reach	does not stop at the position which is safe and keeps moving
confusion	confused (adj) exhibits unclear thoughts
disorientation	disoriented (adj) unsure of correct names of people, place or time
inappropriate	something which is not normal for a particular circumstance

MUST

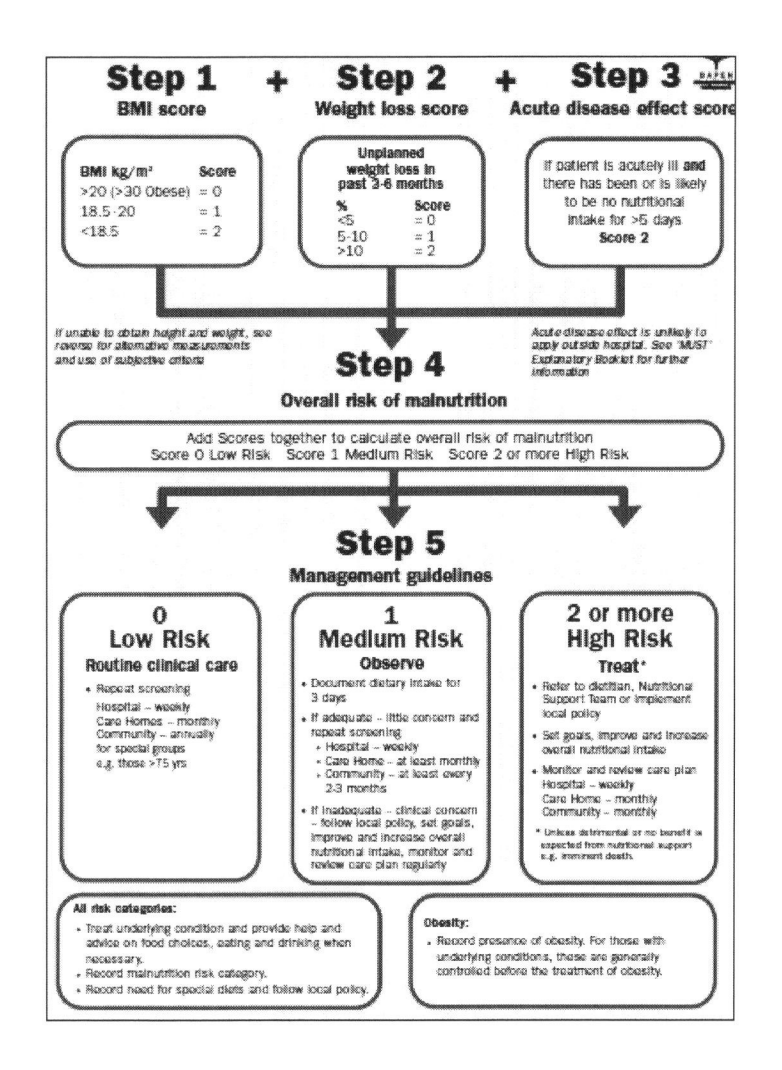

Step 1 — BMI score
BMI kg/m²	Score
>20 (>30 Obese)	= 0
18.5-20	= 1
<18.5	= 2

Step 2 — Weight loss score
Unplanned weight loss in past 3-6 months

%	Score
<5	= 0
5-10	= 1
>10	= 2

Step 3 — Acute disease effect score
If patient is acutely ill **and** there has been or is likely to be no nutritional intake for >5 days
Score 2

If unable to obtain height and weight, see reverse for alternative measurements and use of subjective criteria

Acute disease effect is unlikely to apply outside hospital. See 'MUST' Explanatory Booklet for further information

Step 4 — Overall risk of malnutrition
Add Scores together to calculate overall risk of malnutrition
Score 0 Low Risk   Score 1 Medium Risk   Score 2 or more High Risk

Step 5 — Management guidelines

0 Low Risk — Routine clinical care
- Repeat screening
  Hospital – weekly
  Care Homes – monthly
  Community – annually for special groups e.g. those >75 yrs

1 Medium Risk — Observe
- Document dietary intake for 3 days
- If adequate – little concern and repeat screening
  - Hospital – weekly
  - Care Home – at least monthly
  - Community – at least every 2-3 months
- If inadequate – clinical concern – follow local policy, set goals, improve and increase overall nutritional intake, monitor and review care plan regularly

2 or more High Risk — Treat*
- Refer to dietitian, Nutritional Support Team or implement local policy
- Set goals, improve and increase overall nutritional intake
- Monitor and review care plan
  Hospital – weekly
  Care Home – monthly
  Community – monthly

* Unless detrimental or no benefit is expected from nutritional support e.g. imminent death.

All risk categories:
- Treat underlying condition and provide help and advice on food choices, eating and drinking when necessary.
- Record malnutrition risk category.
- Record need for special diets and follow local policy.

Obesity:
- Record presence of obesity. For those with underlying conditions, these are generally controlled before the treatment of obesity.

score	a number gained after adding up subsections
screen	tests or procedures used to diagnose a disease or condition
dietary intake	the food and drink a patient eats and drinks
special diet	diet for particular conditions e.g low cholesterol diet
obesity	extreme overweight

Oral Assessment

DATE:								
VOICE:	1. Normal 2. Deeper/raspy 3. Difficult speech							
SWALLOW:	1. Normal swallow 2. Difficulty 3. Unable to swallow							
TASTE: (DYSGEUSIA)	1. Normal 2. Impaired/changed 3. No taste							
NON-VERBAL COMMUNICATION: (smiling/grimacing)	1. Normal 2. Difficulty 3. Unable							
LIPS:	1. Smooth, pink, moist 2. Dry/cracked 3. Ulcerated/bleeding							
TONGUE:	1. Pink & moist, papillae present 2. Coated or loss of papillae 3. Blistered/cracked							
SALIVA:	1. Watery 2. Thick or ropy 3. Absent							
MUCOUS MEMBRANES:	1. Pink & moist 2. Reddened/coated 3. Ulcerations with or without bleeding							
GINGIVA:	1. Pink & firm 2. Oedematous with or without redness 3. Spontaneous bleeding							
TEETH/DENTURES:	1. Clean, no debris 2. Localised plaque/debris 3. Generalised plaque/debris							
ANALGESIC REQUIREMENT:	1. None 2. Topical analgesia (difflam/cocaine) 3. Systemic analgesia (diamorphine)							
COMPLICATIONS:	1. No evidence 2. Haemorrhagic mucositis 3. Infection (viral/fungal)							
SELF-CARE ASSESSMENT:	1. Performs mouthcare by self 2. Needs encouragement or education 3. Refuses/unable to perform mouthcare							
TOTAL ORAL ASSESSMENT SCORE								
Initals:								

noun	verb	adjective
rasp	rasp	raspy (voice)
swallowing	swallow	
(sense of) taste	taste	
word		verbal non-verbal (opposite)
communication	communicate	communicative
crack	crack	cracked
ulcer ulceration	ulcerate	ulcerated
bleeding	bleeding	bleeding
papilla (papillae pl)		papillary
blistering	blister	blistered
crack	crack	cracked
saliva	salivate	salivary
coating	coat	coated
water	water	watery
rope		ropy
mucus		mucous
membrane		membranous
redness	redden	reddened
firmness	firm (up)	firm
analgesia	administer an analgesia	analgesic
haemorrhage	haemorrhage	haemorrhagic
infection	infect	infective

Pain Assessment

Words to describe the quality of pain

1	FLICKERING _____	8 TINGLING _____	16 ANNOYING _____
	QUIVERING _____	ITCHY _____	TROUBLESOME _____
	PULSING _____	SMARTING _____	MISERABLE _____
	THROBBING _____	STINGING _____	INTENSE _____
	BEATING _____	9 DULL _____	UNBEARABLE _____
	POUNDING _____	SORE _____	17 SPREADING _____
2	JUMPING _____	HURTING _____	RADIATING _____
	FLASHING _____	ACHING _____	PENETRATING _____
	SHOOTING _____	HEAVY _____	PIERCING _____
3	PRICKING _____	10 TENDER _____	18 TIGHT _____
	BORING _____	TAUT _____	NUMB _____
	DRILLING _____	RASPING _____	DRAWING _____
	STABBING _____	SPLITTING _____	SQUEEZING _____
	LANCINATING _____	11 TIRING _____	TEARING _____
4	SHARP _____	EXHAUSTING _____	19 COOL _____
	CUTTING _____	12 SICKENING _____	COLD _____
	LACERATING _____	SUFFOCATING _____	FREEZING _____
5	PINCHING _____	13 FEARFUL _____	20 NAGGING _____
	PRESSING _____	FRIGHTFUL _____	NAUSEATING _____
	GNAWING _____	TERRIFYING _____	AGONISING _____
	CRAMPING _____	14 PUNISHING _____	DREADFUL _____
	CRUSHING _____	GRUELLING _____	TORTURING _____
6	TUGGING _____	CRUEL _____	*Office Use*
	PULLING _____	VICIOUS _____	S (1-10) _____
	WRENCHING _____	KILLING _____	A (11-15) _____
7	HOT _____	FRIGHTFUL _____	E (16) _____
	BURNING _____	TERRIFYING _____	M (17-20) _____
	SCALDING _____	15 WRETCHED _____	PRI (T) _____
	SEARING _____	BLINDING _____	PPI _____

from the McGill Pain Questionnaire 1971

adjective	verb	noun
flickering	flicker	flickering of
quivering	quiver	quivering
pulsing	pulse	pulse
throbbing	throb	throbbing
beating	beat	beat
pounding	pound	pounding of
jumping	jump	jumping
flashing	flash	flash
shooting	shoot	shot
pricking	prick	prick
boring	bore into	boring
drilling	drill into	drill
stabbing	stab	stabbing
lancinating	lancinate	lancination
pinching	pinch	pinch
pressing	press	pressing
gnawing	gnaw	gnawing
cramping	cramp	cramp
crushing	crush	crushing

adjective	verb	noun
tugging	tug	tugging
pulling	pull	pulling
wrenching	wrench	wrench
hot	heat	heat
burning, burnt	burn	burn
scalding, scalded	scald	scalding
searing	sear	searing
tingling	tingle	tingling
itchy	itch	itch
smarting	smart	smarting
stinging	sting	sting
dull	be dull	dullness
sore	be sore	soreness
hurting	hurt	hurt
aching	ache	ache
heavy	be heavy	heaviness
tender	be tender tenderise	tenderness
taut	be taut	tautness
rasping	rasp	rasp

adjective	verb	noun
splitting	split	split
tiring	tire	tiredness
exhausting	exhaust	exhaustion
sickening	sicken be sick	sickness
suffocating	suffocate	suffocation
fearful	fear	fear
terrifying	terrify be terrified	terror
punishing	punish	punishment
gruelling	be gruelling	
cruel	be cruel	cruelty
vicious	be vicious	viciousness
killing	kill	killing
wretched	be wretched	wretchedness
blinding	blind	blindness
annoying	annoy	annoyance
troublesome	trouble	trouble
miserable	be miserable	misery
intense	be intense	intensity

adjective	verb	noun
unbearable	be unbearable	unbearableness
spreading	spread	spreading
radiating	radiate	radiation
penetrating	penetrate	penetration
piercing	pierce	piercing
tight	be tight	tightness
numb	numb	numbness
drawing	have a drawing pain	
squeezing	squeeze	squeezing
tearing		tear
cool	be cool cool	coolness
cold	be cold	coldness
freezing, frozen	freeze	freezing
nagging	nag	nagging
nauseating	nauseate	nausea
agonising	agonise	agony
dreadful	dread	dread
torturing	torture	torture

Patient Controlled Analgesia

ALLERGIES

ANAESTHETIST _____ (IF UNAVAILABLE, RING ON-CALL ANAESTHETIST)

CONCENTRATION   Use 100ml Bag N/S
                Add _____ mg of MORPHINE / PETHIDINE / FENTANYL
                * NOTE: Remove equal amount of N/S to the ml volume added of Narcotic.

DATE / TIME					
P.C.A. DOSE	MG	MG	MG	MG	MG
LOCKOUT INTERVAL	MIN	MIN	MIN	MIN	MIN
LOADING DOSE	MG	MG	MG	MG	MG
CONTINUOUS RATE	MG/HR	MG/HR	MG/HR	MG/HR	MG/HR
4 HOUR DOSE LIMIT	MG	MG	MG	MG	MG
DOCTORS SIGNATURE					

ALWAYS USE ANTI-REFLUX VALVE ON MAIN I.V. LINE

Connections _____   Purged _____   Checked _____

GENERAL MANAGEMENT
a) Oxygen at _____ litres/min via Hudson Mask / Nasal Cannulae.
b) I.V. access maintained for 3 hours after ceasing P.C.A. infusion.
c) Naloxone 0.4mg available in Ward.
d) No addition narcotics or sedatives to be given except as ordered by the Anaesthetist.
e) Loading dose / Bolus dose - May only be administered by Acute Pain Service (A.P.S.)

OBSERVATIONS
FOR POST-OPERATIVE PATIENTS
- BP, pulse, respiratory rate: 0-2hrs - half-hourly; 2-4hrs - hourly; 4-8hrs - 2 hourly; after 8hrs - 4 hourly.

AFTER CHANGES TO THE ORDERS
- Record BP, pulse, respiratory rate, pain and sedation scores every 15 minutes for half an hour, again in 30 minutes, then resume previous orders.

RECORD RESPIRATION AND SEDATION SCORE
- Every 15 minutes for 1 hour, every 30 minutes for 2 hours, hourly for 2 hours, then 2nd hourly.

noun	verb	adjective
allergy	allergic to	allergic
anaesthetist / anaesthetic	anaesthetise	anaesthetic
lockout	lock out	lockout
load	load (up)	loading
continuation	continue	continuous
connection	connect	connecting
purge of	purge	purging
access	access	access
infusion	infuse	infusing
operation	operate	operative
respiration	respire	respiratory
record	re**cord**	recorded
sedation	sedate	sedative

Oxygen Prescription

Patient details (or addressograph) Name: Date of Birth: Hospital No: Ward / Consultant	In-patient oxygen to be administered (tick) Continuous ☐ Night time ☐ Day time ☐ When required ☐ Target oxygen concentration ___ %	Does patient use oxygen at home (tick) Long Term Oxygen Therapy ☐ Oxygen when required ☐ No home oxygen ☐

		First prescription	Change 1	Change 2	Change 3
State flow rate	Nasal cannulae	1 2 3 4 ...... L/min	1 2 3 4 ...... L/min	1 2 3 4 ...... L/min	1 2 3 4 ...... L/min
	MC (Medium Concentration) mask	1 2 3 4 ...... L/min	1 2 3 4 ...... L/min	1 2 3 4 ...... L/min	1 2 3 4 ...... L/min
	Venturi mask Circle/state concentration required	Concent-ration / Min Flow L/min 24% / 2 28% / 4 35% / 8 40% / 12 60% / 15	Concent-ration / Min Flow L/min	Concent-ration / Min Flow L/min	Concent-ration / Min Flow L/min
	Respiflow State conc. 28-100%	%	%	%	%
State flow rate	Non re-breathing mask (high flow)	L/min	L/min	L/min	L/min
	Non Invasive Ventilation	L/min	L/min	L/min	L/min
	Humidified (if >40%)	Y / N	Y / N	Y / N	Y / N

noun	verb	adjective
in-patient	be an in-patient	in-patient
out-patient	be an out-patient	out-patient
oxygen	oxygenate	oxygenating
	de-oxygenate	de-oxygenating
administration	administer	administered
continuation	continue	continuous
concentration	concentrate	concentrating
therapy		therapeutic
breathing	breathe	breathing
invasion	invade	invasive
humidification	humidify	humidified

VTE

MOBILITY – all patients (tick one box)		
Surgical patient ☐ Medical patient expected to have ongoing reduced mobility relative to normal state ☐		Medical patient **NOT** expected to have significantly reduced mobility relative to normal state ☐
Assess for thrombosis and bleeding risk below		Risk assessment now complete

THROMBOSIS RISK

Patient related	Tick	Admission related	Tick
Active cancer or cancer treatment		Significantly reduced mobility for 3 days or more	
Age > 60		Hip or knee replacement	
Dehydration		Hip fracture	
Known thrombophilias		Total anaesthetic + surgical time > 90 minutes	
Obesity (BMI >30 kg/m2)		Surgery involving pelvis or lower limb with a total anaesthetic + surgical time > 60 minutes	
One or more significant medical co morbidities (e.g. heart disease; metabolic, endocrine or respiratory pathologies; acute infectious diseases; inflammatory conditions)		Acute surgical admission with inflammatory or intra-abdominal condition	
Personal history or first-degree relative with a history of VTE		Critical care admission	
Use of hormone replacement therapy		Surgery with significant reduction in mobility	
Use of oestrogen-containing contraceptive therapy			
Varicose veins with phlebitis			
Pregnancy or < 6 weeks post partum (see NICE guidance for specific risk factors)			

BLEEDING RISK (known or suspected conditions)

Patient related	Tick	Admission related	Tick
Active bleeding		Neurosurgery, spinal surgery or eye surgery	
Acquired bleeding disorders (such as acute liver failure)		Other procedure with high bleeding risk	
Concurrent use of anticoagulants known to increase the risk of bleeding (such as warfarin with INR >2)		Lumbar puncture/epidural/spinal anaesthesia expected within the next 12 hours	
Acute stroke		Lumbar puncture/epidural/spinal anaesthesia within the previous 4 hours	
Thrombocytopaenia (platelets< 75x109/l)			
Uncontrolled systolic hypertension (230/120 mmHg or higher)			
Untreated inherited bleeding disorders (such as haemophilia and von Willebrand's disease)			

noun	verb	adjective
admission discharge (opposite)	admit	admitting
acquisition	acquire	acquired
assessment	assess	assessed
bleeding	bleed	bleeding, blood-stained bloodless (opposite)
coagulation anti-coagulation (opposite)	coagulate	coagulant anticoagulant (opposite)
co-morbidity		co-morbid
concurrence	concur	concurrent
control lack of control (opposite)	control	controlled uncontrolled (opposite)
dehydration hydration (opposite	dehydrate	dehydrating hydrating (opposite)
guidance	guide	guiding
inflammation absence of inflammation	inflame	inflammatory anti-inflammatory (opposite)
medicine		medical
metabolism	metabolise	metabolic
mobility lack of mobility (opposite)	mobilise	mobile immobile (opposite)
puncture	puncture	punctured
replacement	replace	replacing
surgery		surgical
thrombosis	thrombose	thrombolytic
treatment lack of treatment (opposite	treat	treated untreated (opposite)
vein		venous

VIPS

	Score		Stage	Action
IV site appears healthy	0	>	No signs of phlebitis	**OBSERVE CANNULA**
One of the following is evident: • Slight pain near IV site or • Slight redness near IV site	1	>	Possible first signs	**OBSERVE CANNULA**
Two of the following are evident: Pain at IV site • Erythema • Swelling	2	>	Early stage of phlebitis	**RESITE CANNULA**
All of the following signs are evident: • Pain along path of cannula • Erythema • Induration	3	>	Mid-stage of phlebitis	**RESITE CANNULA** **CONSIDER TREATMENT**
All of the following signs are evident and extensive: • Pain along path of cannula • Erythema • Induration • Palpable venous cord	4	>	Advanced stage of phlebitis or start of thrombophlebitis	**RESITE CANNULA** **CONSIDER TREATMENT**
All of the following signs are evident and extensive: • Pain along path of cannula • Erythema • Induration • Palpable venous cord • Pyrexia	5	>	Advanced stage of thrombophlebitis	**INITIATE TREATMENT**

developed by Andrew Jackson, Rotherham General Hospital

noun	verb	adjective
site	site	situated, sited
resite	resite	resited
swelling	swell	swollen
induration	indurate	indurative
palpation	palpate	palpable
pyrexia	be pyrexic	pyrexic

phlebitis	inflammation of the vein
thrombophlebitis	inflammation of a vein caused by a blood clot
erythema	redness
pyrexia	fever, high temperature

Example of an Incident Report

INCIDENT / INJURY REPORT

*To be completed for **ALL** incidents, injuries, accidents and near misses*

Page 1 of 2

Status: ☐ Employee ☐ Visitor ☐ Contractor ☐ Volunteer ☐ Client ☐ Resident ☐ Student

Date:

1. Details of injured person:

Surname:	Phone: (h) (w)
First Name:	Sex: M F
Address:	Date of Birth:
	1st Language:

Experience in job:
- ☐ 0-3 months
- ☐ 4-12 month
- ☐ 1-2 years
- ☐ 3-5 years
- ☐ 5 years plus
- ☐ Casual
- ☐ Permanent P/T
- ☐ Full-time
- ☐ Other

2. Details of witnesses:

Name:	Phone: (h) (w)
Address:	
Name:	Phone: (h) (w)
Address:	

3. Details of incident or accident:

Date: _____ Time of injury: _____

Activity engaged in:

Location of incident / accident:

Describe how and what happened *(please give full details & include a diagram, if appropriate. Use a separate sheet if necessary. Please include car registration number if reporting a Motor Vehicle Accident)*:

4. Details of injury *(the assistance of a supervisor may be required to complete this section)*

Nature of injury / illness (e.g. burn, sprain, cut etc):

How (e.g. fall, grabbed by person, muscular stress):

Location on body (e.g. back, right thumb, left arm etc):

What (e.g. furniture, another person, hot water):

5. Treatment administered:

First Aid Administered:	Yes ☐	No ☐
Treatment:		
Referred to:		
First Aid Attendant (Print Name):	(Signature):	

term	adjective	meaning
adverse incident		unplanned and unwanted occurrence
near miss		an incident which almost happened but was avoided
accident	accidental	an incident which caused an injury
injury (injuries)	injured	damage to the body
1st Language		birth language spoken by a person
contractor	contracted to	a person who works under a contract
volunteer	volunteer	a person who donates their work skills
client	client	a person who receives services
resident	residential	a person who lives in a particular institution
witness /eye witness	witnessed by	a person who actually sees an incident
location	located at /in	place where the incident occurs
report	reported by	written or verbal account of the incident
assistance	assisted by	help to do something
burn	burnt	skin injury caused by fire or chemicals
sprain	sprained	twisting of a muscle
grabbing	grabbed by	holding onto a person often without warning
treatment	treated with	medication or wound dressing after an injury
administration of	administered	the handing out of assistance or medication
First Aid		initial medical treatment done 'on the spot'
referral to	referred to	written or verbal report sent to a second person who is to manage the case

This page to be completed by the Senior Staff Member on duty		
6. Did the injured person stop work:			
Yes ☐ No ☐	If yes, state date:	Time:
Outcome:			
☐ Treated by Doctor	☐ Lodged Workers Comp Claim	☐ Referred to RTW Coordinator
☐ OHS Authority notified	☐ Returned to normal duties	☐ Referred to OHS Coordinator &/or
☒ Hospitalised	☐ Returned to alternative duties	OHS Committee

7. Incident or accident investigation
(Comments to include identified causal factors):

_____
_____
_____
_____

Name & Signature of Supervisor: _____   Date: _____

8. Remedial actions:

☐ Conduct task analysis	☐ Re-instruct persons involved	☐ Improve design / construction / guarding
☐ Conduct hazard systems audit	☐ Improve resident /staff skills mix	☐ Add to inspection program
☐ Develop/ review tasks procedures	☐ Provide debriefing and/or counselling	☐ Improve communication / reporting procedures
☐ Improve work environment	☐ Request maintenance	☐ Improve security
☐ Review OH&S policy/programs	☐ Improve personal protection	☐ Temporarily relocate employees involved
☐ Replace equipment / tools	☐ Improve work congestion/ housekeeping	☐ Falls Prevention Assessment
☐ Improve work organization	☐ Investigate safer alternatives	☐ Request MSDS (Materials Safety Data Sheet)
☐ Develop and/or provide training	☐ Other (specify)	

What, in your own words, has been implemented or planned to prevent recurrence:

_____
_____
_____
_____

9. Remedial actions completed:

Signed (Supervisor): _____ Title: _____ Date: _____

10. Review comments

H.R. Manager: _____

OHS Committee Meeting: _____

_____
_____
_____

Reviewed by CEO / OHS Coordinator (Signed): _____ Date: _____

term	adjective	meaning
completion	completed by	paperwork which is filled in
(on) duty (duties)	dutiful	a work shift
lodgement of a claim (to lodge a claim)	lodged	send in a claim for compensation
coordinator	coordinated by	bring in all relevant people to help with something
notification	notified	let someone know about an incident
hospitalisation	hospitalised	keep a person in hospital for treatment
	alternative	different type of
investigation	investigative	look into the reasons for something
cause	causal	thing or things which made the incident occur
remedy	remedial	do something to make something better
analysis	analyse	check everything to find the cause or causes of the incident
hazard	hazardous	something which is dangerous
construction	constructed with	built using
audit	audited	review a procedure against a standard of care
debriefing (to debrief)	debriefed	talk about an incident afterwards so staff can express their feelings
relocation	relocated	put in a different place
replacement	replaced	exchanged with something new or better
training	trained by	specific workplace course
implementation	implemented by	put into action by

Wound Management Chart

WOUND CHART							
NAME: Mrs A. Patient		DOB: 30/11/1924					
WOUND TYPE	**TICK**	**WOUND APPEARANCE**	**Tick**	**Wound Drainage**	**Tick**	**Pain**	**Tick**
Abrasion		Blister		Purulent (pus)		Site	
Haematoma		Erythema (Redness)		Haemoserous (Blood-stained fluid)		Dressing change	
Laceration		Inflammation		Nil		continuous	
Ulcer		Maceration (over-moist)				intermittent	
Surgical incision		Slough				When limb elevated	
		Eschar (black, hard scab)				Nil	
		Epithelialisation (healing tissue)					

Noun	Verb	Adjective	Meaning
abrasion	abrade	abrasive	graze
chafing	chafe	chafed	skin irritation caused by friction
haematoma			collection of blood under the skin
contusion		contused	bruise
laceration	lacerate	lacerated	cut
ulcer	ulcerate	ulcerated	lesion on or in the skin
incision	incise	incisive	surgical cut
blister	blister	blistering	fluid-filled lesion
erythema		erythmetous	redness
inflammation	inflame	inflamed	red and swollen
maceration	macerate	macerated	excessively moist, soggy
slough	slough off	sloughy	flaky, dead skin
eschar		escharotic	black scab formation
epithelialisation	epithelialise	epithelial	new skin formation, healing
pus	secrete pus	purulent pussy	secretions which are often yellow/green in colour and infective
serum		serous	component of whole blood
intermittence	intermit	intermittent	on and off, not continuous
elevation	elevate	elevated	lift up

Medication

mortar and pestle 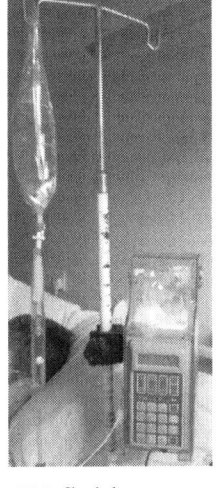 IV fluids  inhaler

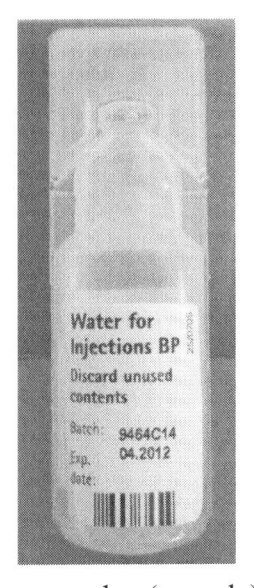

ampoule (ampule) 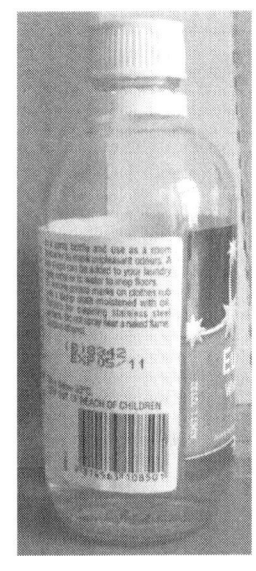 liquid  enema  antiseptic spray

suppository 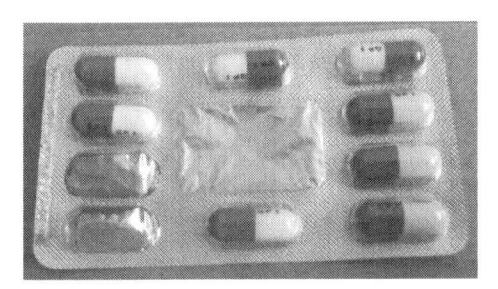 capsule 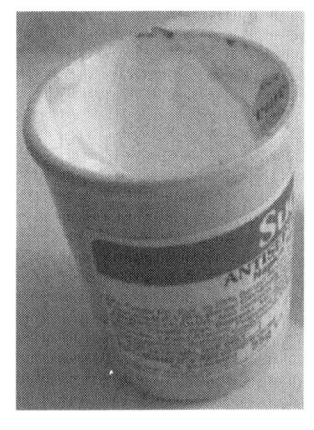 cream

Medication term	Example phrase
ampoule (ampule)	glass ampoule
	plastic ampoule
	snap off the lid of the ampoule
	draw up the ampoule
antibiotics	take a course of antibiotics
	complete the course of antibiotics
antiseptic spray	spray your wound
	spray around your wound
capsule	swallow whole
	don't break open the capsule
	take on an empty stomach
	take with food
	don't take with (name of medication)
contrast medium	inject contrast medium into your cannula
cream	apply some cream
	dab on some cream
	rub in some cream
	rub some cream into your knee
	smother with cream
	use the cream three times a day
	refrigerate the cream after opening
ear wax softener	place a few drops into the outer ear canal
	plug the outer ear with some cotton wool
effervescent tablet	dissolve the tablet in water before taking
eye drops	instil the drops twice a day
	instil / put the drops into the lower conjunctival sac
	cover your eye with an eye pad and shield
	the drops may make your vision blurry
	the drops will dilate your pupils
	discard one month after opening

eye ointment	squeeze the ointment into the lower conjunctival sac
	use the eye ointment at night because your vision will be blurry
elixir	take the cough elixir when needed
	take internally
enema	insert the enema into your rectum (back passage)
	put the enema into your rectum
	hold the enema fluid for fifteen minutes if you can
gargle	gargle three times a day
	do not swallow
inhaler	depress /push down the canister
	breathe in the aerosol
injection	draw up an injection
	give an injection into your thigh
	give an injection into your tummy / abdomen
IV injection	inject medication into the cannula in your vein
IV fluids	put up / hang a bag of IV fluids
	start an IV infusion
	infuse the IV fluids through a pump
(medication) liquid	swallow the liquid
(cleansing) liquid	swab the area with the liquid
	dab the antiseptic around the wound
	irrigate the wound with saline
	cleanse the wound with the saline
	flush the eye with clean water
lozenge	suck the lozenge slowly
	do not chew the lozenge
mouthwash	gargle with the mouthwash to freshen the breath

nasal spray	put the canister into one nostril and block the other
	press down the canister
	don't blow your nose for a few minutes after using the spray
nebule	snap off the top of the nebule before use
	squeeze the contents of the nebule into the nebuliser chamber
	breathe in the nebuliser mist
patch	apply the patch to a clean area of skin
	stick the patch onto a clean area of skin
peppermint water	sip the peppermint water to relieve indigestion
	do not swallow all at once
pessary	insert the pessary high up into your vagina
(antiseptic) powder	sprinkle powder onto the wound
(medication) powder	dissolve the powder in a little water before taking
	dissolve all the powder in the ampoule before drawing up
saline flush	give a saline flush
	flush your cannula
sublingual tablet	put the table under your tongue and allow it to dissolve without chewing
suspension	shake the suspension well before taking
	measure in a measuring cup or measuring syringe
tablet	don't crush the tablet
	crush the tablet using a mortar and pestle
	take on an empty stomach
	take with food
	take on an empty stomach
	take with food
tincture	paint on the tincture

Manual Handling

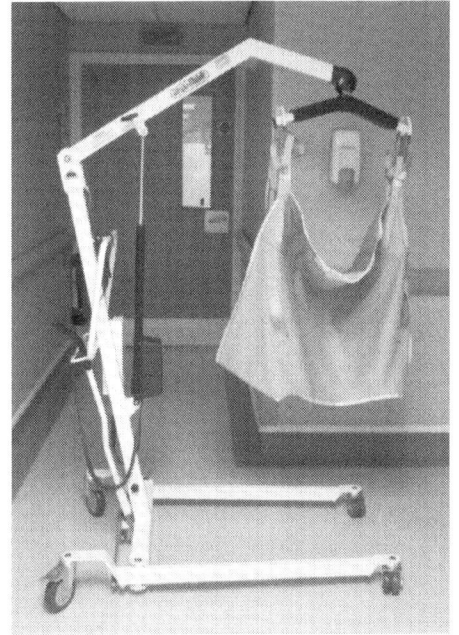

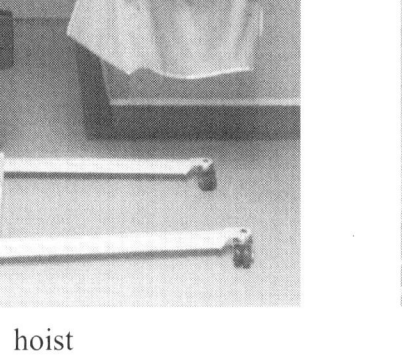

hoist

slide sheet

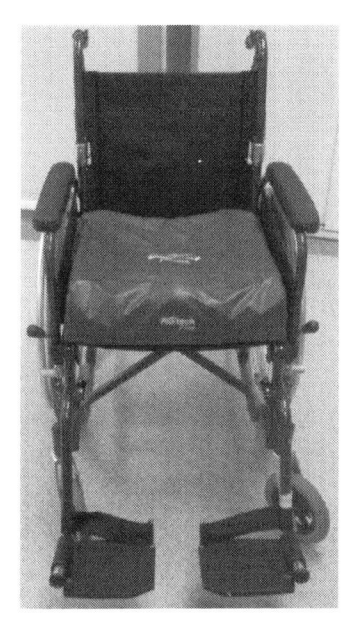

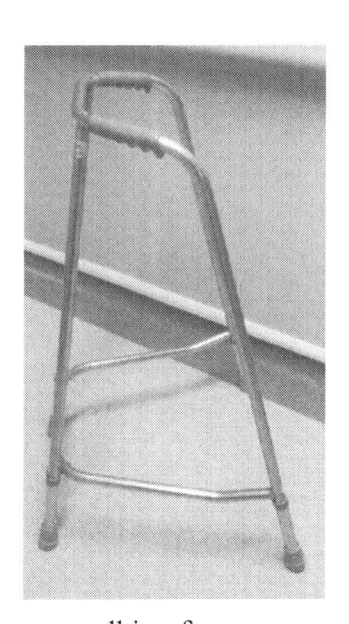

wheelchair

walking frame

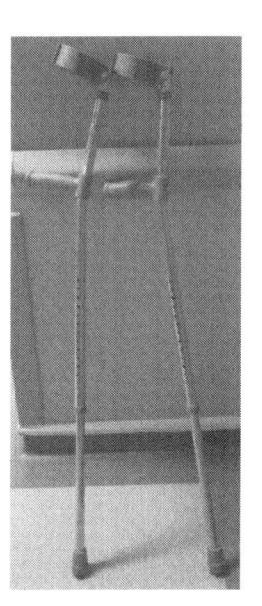

crutches

term	meaning
manual handling	moving equipment and people using equipment or special techniques (from *manus* = hand), Also, *patient handling*
hoist	equipment used to lift heavy and immobilised patients
hoist sling	a fabric hammock which cradles the patient during hoisting
slide sheet	slippery material placed under a patient to help with movement in a bed or chair
sit to stand hoist	a hoist which helps patients contribute to standing from a sitting position
alternating pressure mattress	air mattress whose pressure levels change continuously
profiling bed	bed with sections which can be adjusted independently of the other sections
mobility aids	equipment which helps a person who is unsteady to move around
handling belt	a wide belt with handles which patients wear to give staff a handle to grip to keep patients steady when mobilising
wheelchair	a chair on wheels which is used by patients who are unable to walk
walking frame	also called *Zimmer frame* or *gait frame*, equipment which gives unsteady patients a place to hold onto when walking
forearm crutches	sticks which help steady patients when they mobilise especially after orthopaedic surgery

Patient Handling Considerations

Consider all factors that could affect the patient's mobility including:
1. **Relevant medical history**, e.g. CVA, arthritis, amputation, Parkinson's Disease, osteoporosis etc.
2. **Physical disabilities**, e.g. eye sight, hearing, speech
3. **Psychological** e.g. confused, aggression etc
   - Fully co-operative – able to conform and maintain mobility
   - Comatosed – completely unable to comprehend any verbal commands and unable to conform
   - Confused and unable to understand – patients who cannot comprehend what is expected of them and unable to determine how they can help
   - Agitated – disturbed or excitable. State of mind which may make manual handling difficult
   - Aggressive – the patient may have unprovoked hostility and the intention to harm others
4. **Pain status**
5. **Tissue Viability**
6. **History of fall(s)** – does the patient have any previous history of falling to the ground, past or present:
   History of vertigo – does the patient have a feeling of themselves or the surroundings rotating, spinning or have they any balance problems?
   - Low haemoglobin – to the best of your knowledge does the patient have low haemoglobin, which may precipitate fainting or falling?
   - Spasms/Epilepsy – does the person have uncontrolled limb jerks and involuntary muscle contraction and rigidity they may or may not be aware of?
   - Other – please highlight any other medical history which may predetermine manual handling problems i.e. dizziness, faintness
   - Cultural/religious considerations
   - Day/Night variations (does the patients physical/mental capabilities fluctuate during the day necessitating differing levels of assistance or equipment?)
   - Attachments, e.g.. IV lines, catheter, oxygen therapy etc.

relevant	information which relates to the topic
arthritis	inflammatory disease of the joints
amputation	removal of a limb or body part leaving a stump
osteoporosis	bone thinning disease
co-operative	patients help staff with the move or mobilising
comatosed	unconscious and unable to respond to requests to move
agitated	nervous and sometimes flailing arms about
aggressive	attempting to fight or physically lash out
pain status	whether pain is mild, moderate or severe
tissue viability	whether a patient has a wound or skin issue (e.g fragile skin)
vertigo	dizziness
haemoglobin	oxygen-carrying part of the blood
spasm	painful and unexpected twisting of a muscle
epilepsy	fitting
faintness	brief blackouts not related to epilepsy
attachments	any tubes or drains in situ (in place)

Manual Handling Training

Task	No of staff	Equipment Used	Method
Turning in bed			
Moving up/down bed			
Sitting up in bed			
In and out of bed			
Transfer bed to trolley			
Transferring bed to chair			
Chair to chair			
Repositioning in chair			
Transferring chair to bed			
Standing			
Mobilising			
Toileting			
Bathing/washing			

palmar grip	clasping the hand of the patient to support patient
lateral transfer	move from bed to chair or chair to wheelchair (side to side)
reposition in chair	adjust a patient's posture when sitting in a chair
sitting to the bed edge	assist a patient to sit with legs over the edge of the bed
rolling to one side	changing from flat on the back to lying on one side
transfer weight	lean most of the body weight on one side of the body
fold slide sheet under the patient	double a slide sheet and tuck under the patient
support the patient's trunk	hold a slide sheet firmly at the level of the patient's waist
tuck your chin onto your chest	position your chin downwards as far as it will go
'Ready, steady, go'	the command made before moving a patient
lie prone	lie flat on your back looking at the ceiling
lie supine	lie flat on your abdomen facing the floor
bariatric patients	patients who are extremely obese, >127kg

Dental terms

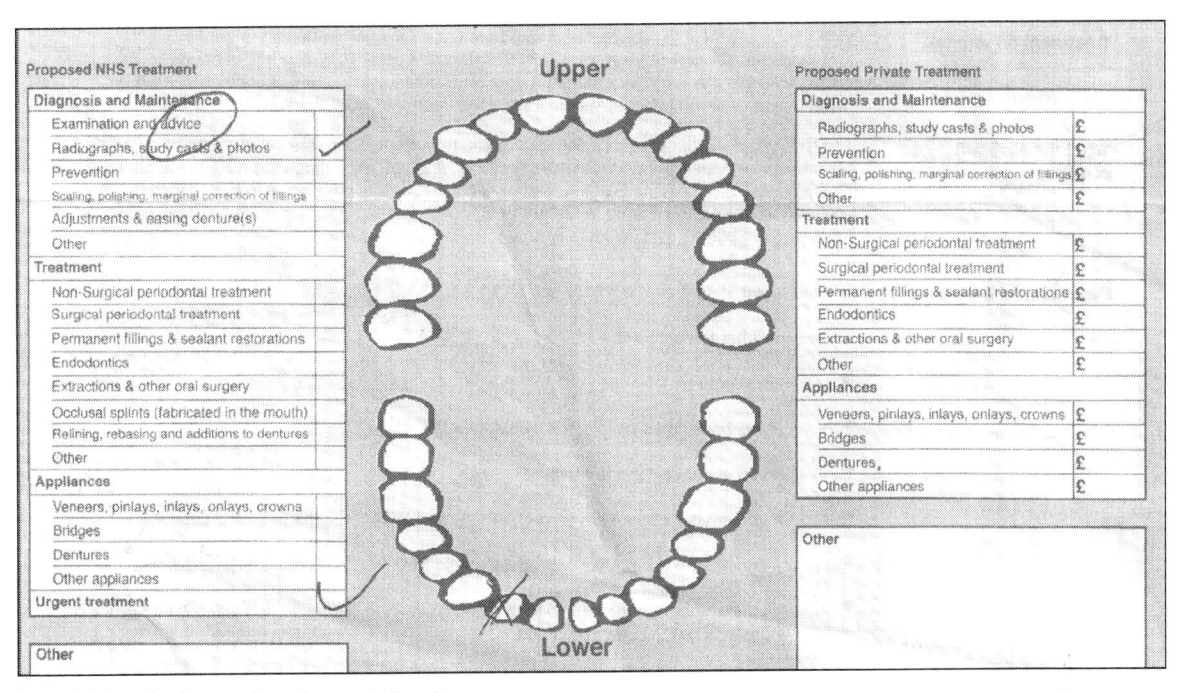

from: Virginia Allum dental record 2012

term	adjective	meaning
dentistry	dental	care of the teeth and gums
endodontics	endodontal	care of the root and pulp of the tooth
pedodontist	pedodontal	dentist specialising in the care of children's teeth
periodontics	periodontal	care of the gums
examination	examined by	to look at the teeth and gums
study cast		make a model of the teeth
prevention	prevented	stop something from happening
scaling	scaled	chip off hard pieces of plaque
polishing	polished	shine the outside of the tooth
filling	filled	insertion of material to plug a hole
adjustment	adjusted	change slightly so it is more comfortable
sealant	sealed	covering which prevents liquid or infective agents being able to enter the tooth

term	adjective	meaning
impression		a mould taken to check a person's bite
extraction	extracted	pull out a tooth
splint	splinted	implement which holds teeth in place
occlusal splint	occlusal	mouth guard worn at night to protect against clenching of teeth
dental appliances	dental	any devices worn in the mouth
denture		set of false teeth
veneer	veneeral	layer of material attached to the front of the tooth
pinlay		restoration of the crown and root of a tooth
inlay	inlayed	small piece of material stuck onto the tooth to restore the surface of the tooth
onlay		restoration which covers the whole of the tooth surface
crown	crowned	artificial covering stuck onto the tooth
implant	implanted	permanent replacement of a missing tooth
molar		last three upper and lower teeth
wisdom tooth		third molar tooth
deciduous teeth	deciduous	baby teeth, first teeth which fall out
root canal treatment		removal of the nerve of a decayed tooth and replacement with a filling
caries		dental decay
gingivitis		inflammation and infection of the gums
bruxism		tooth grinding
calculus		hard deposits on teeth. also called tartar

term	adjective	meaning

Printed in Great Britain
by Amazon